Eighty years after the Battles of El Alamein it's hard to imagine how close the Axis powers came to victory. For almost six months the two sides wrestled like lions, the Axis needing to secure Suez to open a supply line to the southern USSR whilst blocking the Allies' south-eastern passages, while the Allies needed Suez to maintain a passage for troops and material, including vital oil supplies, as well as to continue the fight against Imperial Japan.

The Battles of El Alam ————— —— ——d by the Qattara Depression, with its salt l with the Mediterranean boundary. This meant t the other en masse, tho sides regularly used the defensive positions bui and running north to sc....

German prisoners wait for transport at El Alamein, 25 October 1942. (IWM)

Not all challenges came from the enemy. A wall of sand approaches Allied lines late in October 1942. (IWM)

Armourers prepare to load 250lb GP bombs onto the Kittyhawks of 260 Squadron, RAF. Note the truck at the head of the trolleys with its tripod Browning machine-gun mount. (IWM)

Memorial to the 9th Australian Division at the El Alamein Cemetery. (Unknown)

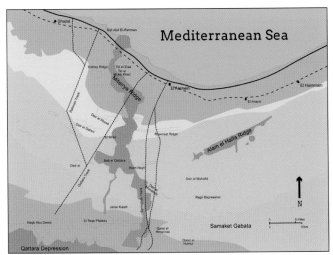

Map showing the features that were to play so prominent a role in the coming battles.

Troops also had to face the daily threats of heat, thirst and scorpions, as well as the Sirocco carrying fine sand that reduced visibility and affected engines. For the Axis their problems were compounded by a logistics network constantly under attack, and having to use captured stores to continue their advance. For the Allies, fighting the Deutsches Afrikakorps would highlight shortcomings in organization that would be equally costly. For both sides the stakes were as high as they could be.

In the end the Allies excelled themselves. Superb leadership, sound intelligence and planning, coupled with better equipment and service support as well as greater numbers turned the tide against the Axis forces decisively.

Today signs of battle remain; abandoned dugouts, empty fuel cans and unexploded ordnance abound. It's almost impossible to imagine that an army on the cusp of defeat in early summer 1942 could achieve so complete a victory six months later.

1

THE BATTLES OF EL ALAMEIN

The Battles of El Alamein featured well-known and notable commanders on all sides; however there are three whose names and influence have become the stuff of legend: Auchinleck, Montgomery and Rommel.

The genesis of El Alamein was formed almost 18 months previously in the destruction of the Italian Tenth Army by General Archibald Wavell and his Western Desert Force as part of Operation Compass. The German Oberkommando der Wehrmacht (OKW – Armed Forces High Command) felt that the Italians needed support to stop the Allied advance westwards and to prevent the loss of the strategically valuable North African front. The commander chosen to lead this new force would become synonymous with the desert campaign; Johannes Erwin Eugen Rommel.

Known as the 'Desert Fox', Rommel was a career soldier who had served with the German Army since 1910. Between the wars he served in a range of command and staff posts and published *Infanterie greift an* (*Infantry Attacks*), a study of his experiences as an infantry commander during the First World War.

Promoted to Generalmajor in August 1939 Rommel commanded the Führerbegleitbatallion (FBB – Führer Escort Brigade) during the invasion of Poland, where he was able to witness the effects of Blitzkrieg for himself. As a result of lobbying Rommel was given command of 7th Panzer Division. In early 1940 he started to prepare his new division for operations in the West. During the battles for the Low Countries and France Rommel was never far from the front line and on one occasion took up arms himself, helping to repel a French counter-attack. Rommel's drive rubbed off on his division and it earned itself the nickname 'Gespensterdivision' ('Ghost Division') as the Oberkommando des Heeres (OKH – German Army High Command) rarely knew its precise location due to the speed of its advance. With this tactical élan it was clear Rommel was becoming a master of Blitzkrieg.

On 6 February 1941 Rommel was appointed commander of the new Deutsches Afrikakorps (DAK), formed from 5th Light Division, which later became 21st Panzer Division, and 15th Panzer Division. Three days later Rommel was promoted to Generalleutnant, and on 12 February arrived in Tripoli subordinated to Italian commander-in-chief General Italo Gariboldi. His arrival was part of Unternehmen Sonnenblume or Operation Sunflower, the name given to the deployment of German forces to North Africa.

General Sir Claude Auchinleck, known as 'The Auk', replaced General Sir Archibald Wavell after the failure of Operation Battleaxe, the relief of Tobruk, in June 1941. Auchinleck was a product of the British Indian Army, having been commissioned into the 62nd Punjabis in 1904. At the outbreak of the Second World War Auchinleck was appointed to command the Indian 3rd Infantry Division followed by command of IV Corps in January 1940 and a subsequent promotion to lieutenant general. He went on to command the Anglo-French ground

Rommel in conference. The desert was a tactician's dream and Rommel ensured he utilized this canvas to the fullest in his drives eastwards. (German Federal Archives)

Rommel (third from right), with the 25th Panzer Regiment during the Western campaign in June 1940; second from left Colonel Karl Rothenburg: Hauptmann Schulz, Chief of 1st Battalion of the 25th Panzer Regiment. (German Federal Archives)

forces in the ill-fated Norwegian campaign. Upon his return to the UK Auchinleck took command of V Corps, before moving to Southern Command. By the end of 1940 Auchinleck had been promoted to full general and Commander-in-Chief India.

General Sir Archibald Wavell, Commander-in-Chief India, and General Sir Claude Auchinleck, Commander-in-Chief Middle East, in conference on 8 September 1941. (IWM)

Auchinleck's first taste of the war in the Middle East occurred in April 1941 with the defence of RAF Habbaniya in Iraq, which was under threat by the pro-Axis regime led by Arab Nationalist Ali al-Gaylan. At the time Wavell was unable to spare troops, so acting on his own initiative Auchinleck dispatched a battalion from the King's Own Royal Regiment by air with the Indian 10th Infantry Division following by sea. By the time a relief column from Habfor (Habbaniya Force) arrived from the British Mandate of Palestine, the short-lived Anglo-Iraqi war was over.

Major General John 'Jock' Campbell VC, commanding officer 7th Armoured Division, with Auchinleck. (IWM)

Down but not out. Later in the war Ritchie would command XII Corps in France. (IWM)

In July 1941 Auchinleck replaced Wavell as Commander-in-Chief Middle East and wasted no time taking the fight to the Axis, launching Operation Crusader in November 1941 to relieve the garrison at Tobruk. Crusader was a disaster, however, Auchinleck's lack of experience in using armour leading to five times as many tank losses as those experienced by the Axis. Within six months the Axis were in the ascendancy, taking Tobruk and driving the Allies back into Egypt, where Auchinleck managed to stem their advance at El Alamein.

By the summer of 1942 his position as Commander-in-Chief Middle East and acting General Officer Commanding Eighth Army, having relieved its original commander General Neil Ritchie in June, was untenable. He was relieved of his command in August, and returned to India.

With the roles of Commander-in-Chief Middle East and General Officer Commanding Eighth Army once again split, General Sir Harold Alexander became Commander-in-Chief Middle East and Lieutenant General William Gott took command of the Eighth Army. Sadly Gott's appointment was

General Sir Harold Alexander, pictured here in August 1942 as Commander-in-Chief, Middle East, surveys the battlefront from an open car. To his right is Major General John Harding, Deputy Director of Military Training Middle East Command. (IWM)

Captain Bernard Montgomery DSO with a fellow officer of 104th Infantry Brigade, 35th Division. Montgomery was awarded the DSO for conspicuous gallantry on 13 October 1914 during the Battle of the Aisne in which he was wounded. (IWM)

Auchinleck in command of the Eighth Army arrived. Hitting the ground running, the new appointment was a great believer in Generalissimo Alexander Suvorov's adage 'Train hard, fight easy'. A man who respected the enemy but was resolved to beat them: Lieutenant General Bernard Law Montgomery.

Montgomery had been originally commissioned in the Royal Warwick Regiment in 1908, though barely as he was expelled for fighting and rowdiness during his studies at the Royal Military College Sandhurst. During the First World War Montgomery was wounded twice and awarded the Distinguished Service Order. Between the wars various command and staff appointments followed, including tours in Palestine and India. As Officer Commanding 9th Infantry Brigade Montgomery arranged an amphibious combined operations exercise for the new Commander-in-Chief of Southern Command, General Sir Archibald Wavell. This experience would serve Montgomery well in the war years.

In 1939 Montgomery took command of 3rd (Iron) Infantry Division, deploying to Belgium as part of the British Expeditionary Force (BEF). During the Phoney War period Montgomery pushed his men hard, ensuring training and discipline was maintained. As a result his division had the best performance of any British unit during the Battle of France and the subsequent withdrawal of the BEF. Montgomery's persistence and high standards had paid dividends. It was during Operation Dynamo, the evacuation from Dunkirk, that Montgomery assumed command of II Corps from Lieutenant General Sir Alan Brooke.

On his return to the UK Montgomery was given the command of V Corps, and busied himself with preparations for the defence of Hampshire and Dorset, where he worked under Auchinleck. The working relationship between the two was far from congenial and the effects continued long after the two parted ways. In 1941 Montgomery took command of XII Corps. Based in Kent, this was subsequently extended to cover Sussex and Surrey. He continued to push his troops hard, demanding excellence in terms of physical fitness and capacity. To engender an offensive spirit he renamed his command the South-Eastern Army, holding an impressive combined-arms exercise involving over 100,000 troops in May 1942. During this time he was promoted to lieutenant general.

Arriving in theatre on 13 August 1942, Montgomery's drive and experience would help the Allies turn a corner and leave the Germans with their first major defeat at the hands of the Western Allies.

short-lived, as he killed when his aircraft was shot down en-route to take over his new command.

As a result the man originally favoured by Chief of the Imperial General Staff, General Sir Alan Brooke, to take over from

A portrait of Montgomery taken during a visit to England in 1943. (IWM)

Watching the advance. Montgomery's personal drive made him a favourite of the men, but the bane of his fellow officers. (HMSO)

For brevity the ORBAT of all sides has been broken down to corps and divisional level only. Commanders listed were effective 23 October 1942.

AXIS FORCES

Panzerarmee Afrika – Generalfeldmarschall Johannes Erwin Eugen Rommel

Deutsches Afrika Korps – Generalleutnant Wilhelm Ritter von Thoma

15th Panzer Division – Generalmajor Gustav von Vaerst
21st Panzer Division – Generalmajor Heinz von Randow
90th Light Division – Generalleutnant Theodor Graf von Sponeck

Italian Army Africa – Marshal Ettore Bastico

16th Motorised Division Pistoia – Generale di Divisione Giuseppe Falugi

136th Armoured Division Giovani Fascisti – Generale di Divisione Ismaele Di Nisio

Italian X Army Corps, Army Corps – Generale di Corpo d'armata Edoardo Nebbia:

17th Infantry Division Pavia – Generale di Divisione Nazzareno Scattaglia
27th Infantry Division Brescia – Generale di Divisione Brunetto Brunetti
185th Infantry Division 'Folgore' – Generale di Divisione Enrico Frattini
Ramcke Parachute Brigade – Generalmajor Hermann-Bernhard Ramcke

Italian XX Army Corps – Generale di Corpo d'armata Giuseppe de Stephanis:

101st Motorised Division Trieste – Generale di Divisione Francisco La Ferla
132nd Armoured Division Ariete – Generale di Divisione Francesco Arena
133rd Armoured Division Littorio – Generale di Divisione Gervasio Bitossi
German 164th Light Africa Division – Generalleutnant Carl-Hans Lungershausen

Italian XXI Army Corps, Generale di Corpo d'armata Enea Navarini:

25th Infantry Division Bologna Alessandro Gloria
102nd Motorised Division Trento – Generale di Divisione Giorgio Masina

Luftflotte 2 – Generalfeldmarschall Albert Kesselring

Fliegerführer Afrika – General der Flieger Hans Seidemann

Sturzkampfgeschwader 3
Jagdgeschwader 27
Jagdgeschwader 53
Lehrgeschwader 1
Desert Emergency Squadron 1
Courier Squadron Africa
Luftgaustab z.b.V. Africa
Air Force News Regiment Africa

ALLIED FORCES

Commander-in-Chief Middle East – General the Hon. Sir Harold Alexander

Eighth Army – Lieutenant General Sir Bernard Montgomery

X Corps – Lieutenant General Herbert Lumsden:

1st Armoured Division, including Hammerforce – Major General Harold Briggs
8th Armoured Division – Major General Charles Gairdner
10th Armoured Division – Major General Alexander Gatehouse

XIII Corps – Lieutenant General Brian Horrocks:

7th Armoured Division (inc. Free French Brigade – Brigadier Marie Pierre Koenig) – Major General Allan Harding
44th (Home Counties) Infantry Division – Major General Ivor Hughes
50th (Northumbrian) Infantry Division (inc. 1st Greek Infantry Brigade – Colonel Pausanias Katsotas) – Major General John Nicols

XXX Corps – Lieutenant General Sir Oliver Leese:

9th Australian Division – Major General Leslie Morshead
51st Highland Infantry Division – Major General Douglas Wimberley
2nd New Zealand Division – Lieutenant General Bernard Freyberg
1st South African Division – Major General Dan Pienaar
4th Indian Infantry Division – Major General Francis Tucker

There were also various specialist units that fell under direct Army, Corps and Divisional command such as Royal Corps of Signals detachments.

Western Desert Air Force – Air Vice-Marshal Arthur Coningham, RAF

The Western Desert Air Force (WDAF) was subordinated to General Headquarters RAF Middle East commanded by Air Chief Marshal Sir William Mitchell. The following units supported ground operations on 27 October 1942:

No. 3 South African Air Force (SAAF) Bomber Wing – Colonel Henry Martin SAAF
No. 232 Bomber Wing
No. 285 Reconnaissancc Wing
No. 211 Group – Air Vice Marshal Harry Broadhurst:
No. 233 Wing
No. 239 Wing
No. 244 Wing

No. 212 Group – Group Captain Harold Fenton:
No. 243 Wing
No. 7 Wing

US Desert Air Task Force

The US Desert Air Task Force fell under WDAF operational control, with the exception of 81st Bombardment Squadron, part of 12th Bombardment Group.

57th Fighter Group USAAF
12th Bombardment Group USAAF
Air Ambulance Squadron
835th Aviation Engineer Battalion

Defeat is one thing; disgrace is another. Nothing could exceed the sympathy and chivalry of my two friends. There were no reproaches; not an unkind word was spoken. 'What can we do to help?' said Roosevelt. I replied at once, 'Give us as many Sherman tanks as you can spare and ship them to the Middle East as quickly as possible.'

Winston Churchill, 21 June 1942.

A Panzerjäger-Abteilung, part of 21st Panzer Division, on the move. (Georg Weber)

When Rommel established his headquarters at Hotel Tobruk on 21 June 1942, the sense of triumph must have been overwhelming. The Battle of Gazala and the fall of Tobruk were the latest defeats for a year of turmoil in the British Empire. Auchinleck, on the other hand, must have been furious, for he had lost Tobruk with its much-needed garrison of 35,000 men along with two months' worth of supplies.

As a result the Eighth Army was forced to withdraw beyond 'The Wire', the border between Italian Libya and British Egypt, to the small town of Mersa Matruh. This withdrawal became known as the 'Gazala Gallop', due its speed to save as much material as possible. By 29 June Mersa Matruh had fallen into Italian hands, along with its 6,000-strong garrison and supplies that were soon put to use driving Panzerarmee Afrika eastwards once more.

Eyes west. Allied infantry in defensive positions waiting for the arrival of Panzerarmee Afrika. (UK Govt)

The race for Suez was on, with Axis and Allied forces often overtaking one another, dashing headlong for safety or victory. Rommel tried to cut off the Eighth Army's withdrawal by ordering the Afrika Korps southwards. However, this proved harder than expected as a result of the Afrika Korps using a vast amount of captured equipment (some estimates put the figure at 85 percent of the motor pool). The ensuing confusion between friend and foe worked in the Allies' favour, yet Rommel continued his advance eastwards.

Rommel passing Commonwealth prisoners in Tobruk with DAK Chief of Staff Fritz Bayerlein. (German Federal Archives)

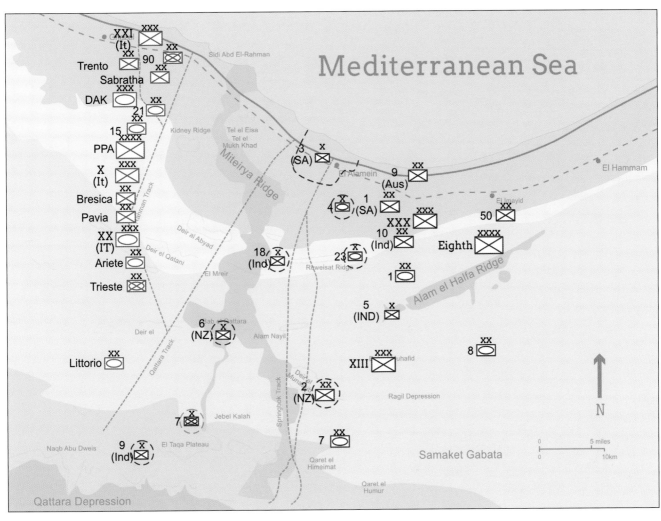

In a man to man fight, the winner is he who has one more round within himself.

Rommel

By the end of June 1942 both sides had been fighting hard in 35°C heat and the Eighth Army was truly on the back foot. Its commander Ritchie was removed on 25 June, with Auchinleck taking over. The Eighth Army could muster just over 130 serviceable tanks with a further 950 in repair behind the lines. The situation was grim indeed, with defeat seemingly a matter of time. However, the key word was *seemingly*.

Auchinleck had withdrawn to prepared defensive positions where he was able to access fresh troops and materiel. A

definitive defensive line had been drawn in the sand starting at a small railway halt 260km (162 miles) from Cairo, whose name would become synonymous with both the Eighth Army and its most famous commander Montgomery; El Alamein.

The Qattara Depression was a mere 65km (40 miles) south of El Alamein, its close proximity allowing Auchinleck to channel and to some extent control the movements of the advancing Panzerarmee Afrika. The British withdrawal had also shortened their supply lines, with reinforcements and replacement stores being unloaded a mere 120km (75 miles) away, while to the west

German infantry advancing towards the Egyptian border. (Library of Congress)

Planning a rain of fire. The command post of 83rd and 85th Batteries, 11th Field Regiment, Royal Artillery at El Alamein, July 1942. (IWM)

7

An RAF Lysander flies over a convoy during the withdrawal into Egypt, 26 June 1942. (IWM)

the newly-promoted Rommel found himself wanting an extra Panzer division rather than his field marshal's baton.

Rommel may have gained ground courtesy of captured stores but the further east he pushed the more stretched his supply lines became. The capture of the strategic port of Tobruk was not as helpful as it might have been, since its cargo-handling equipment had been heavily damaged and the port was unable to work to full capacity. Rommel also faced reduced air cover from the Luftwaffe and Regia Aeronautica as both struggled to find suitable areas to fly from. Meanwhile Allied interceptions of Axis shipping in the Mediterranean meant that Rommel was almost constantly operating below his monthly requirement of 70,000 tons of supplies.

With the capture of Tobruk Rommel had intended to give Panzerarmee Afrika respite, to refit before pushing on, but the crumbling British offensive spirit at both Gazala and Mersa Matruh had boosted his confidence. He was also aware that any pause, no matter how short, would give Auchinleck the chance to build up his reserves of men and material via Alexandria and Port Said. This prompted Rommel to continue his advance, using captured stores picked up along the way to maintain his offensive. By 29 June Rommel was ready to take the fight to the Eighth Army; he would repeat his wide sweeping manoeuvre that had been extraordinarily effective at Gazala and Mersa Matruh.

Prior preparation and planning. Eighth Army equipment being removed from Mersa Matruh, 26 June 1942. (IWM)

Field Marshal Erwin Rommel drawing up plans, 1942. (German Federal Archives)

Auchinleck planned to engage Panzerarmee Afrika on the defensive line where he had arranged his defences in a series of 'Boxes', defensive pockets which varied in size from brigade to corps. These were established at key points with infantry and artillery along with mobile assets that would engage enemy forces that managed to break through the line.

Meanwhile in Alexandria and Cairo the situation was one of disarray, with civil servants destroying files and Middle East

A 25pdr field gun of 11th Field Regiment, Royal Artillery, in action during the First Battle of El Alamein, July 1942. (IWM)

Ready for the off. A Panzer II awaits the order to move. Note the DAK symbol next to the driver's viewport. (German Federal Archives)

Headquarters moving to Palestine. The Mediterranean Fleet dispersed to Beirut and Haifa, and plans for the destruction of ports and cargo-handling facilities were drawn up.

On 1 July Rommel struck, with 90th Light Division leading the way. His plan was to bypass Lieutenant General Charles Norrie's XXX Corps' box network around El Alamein, cutting it off before swinging south towards Alam Nayil and taking the fight to Gott's XIII Corps. The Italians would then attack El Alamein from the west with General Alessandro Gloria's XXI Corps, and General Giuseppe De Stefani's XX Corps following the Deutsches Afrika Korps (DAK) before swinging southwards towards Victoria Cross holder Lieutenant General Bernard Freyberg's New Zealand 2nd Division at Bab el Qattara.

The moment Panzerarmee Afrika's 90th Light Division left their start lines Rommel's plan began to falter, even before first contact with the Eighth Army. A combination of poor light and a sandstorm disorientated the attacking panzergrenadiers who ended up engaging with Auchinleck's well-prepared defenders. These encounters slowed the advance down initially, though by mid-afternoon it had resumed. Elsewhere the 15th and 21st Panzer Divisions had attracted the attentions of Air Vice Marshall Arthur Coningham's Western Desert Air Force (WDAF) as they approached their line of departure. These attacks, combined with having to pass over difficult terrain, meant their H-hour was delayed by three hours.

Almost immediately they ploughed headlong into the 18th Indian Infantry Brigade which had arrived from Mosul with a mere 48 hours to prepare their positions at Deir el Shein, in

Preparing to engage. A firepower demonstration by a Hawker Hurricane of 6 Squadron RAF with its Vickers 40mm Type S anti-tank guns against derelict German tanks. (IWM)

front of the Ruweisat Ridge. The 18th were part of the larger South African 1st Division and were able to combine the South Africans' artillery fire with their own against the advancing DAK troops. Their commander, General der Panzertruppe Walther Nehring, a veteran of Operation Barbarossa, was taken completely by surprise. According to intelligence the 18th Brigade should not have been there. However, Nehring was fully engaged and determined to see the action through. By that evening his panzer divisions gained the upper hand and had overwhelmed the 18th, smashing it into near oblivion. The cost was high, however; he had lost eighteen of his fifty-five tanks. To the north the 90th Light Division still struggled, attracting attention from the South African gunners. Such was the weight of fire that the advance ceased and they were caught in the open, along with Rommel, for three hours.

Auchinleck's plan was working and the support given to him by the WDAF was making a difference, and combined with the efforts of the South Africans and the 18th Indian Brigade he was able to muster fresh troops who would be able to begin repelling Panzerarmee Afrika's advances. XXX Corps was ordered to stop Rommel's advance, and allow XIII Corps to advance northward and slam into his right flank with armour, attacking either side of the Ruweisat Ridge. At the same time the New Zealanders would leave their positions at Bab el Qattara and Naqb au Dweis and, alongside the Indian 5th Division, prepare for a mobile role.

Major General Bernard Freyberg (centre right), arriving to conduct a review of 6th Brigade, is greeted by the commander of 24th Battalion, Lieutenant Colonel Clayden Shuttleworth (left), and Brigadier Harold Barrowclough, September 1941. Freyberg's New Zealanders would earn a fearsome reputation for their determination during the Desert Campaign. (IWM)

The following day the 90th Light Division was still under artillery fire and Rommel realized it needed support to continue its advance. Nehring was ordered to detach some of his armour to support the bogged-down 90th. Ironically the strengthened DAK advance coincided with the Eighth Army's counter-attack onto the Ruweisat Ridge resulting in fierce fighting carrying on until nightfall. The tanks of Lieutenant General Herbert Lumsden's 1st Armoured Division were held in check by DAK anti-tank guns, and Nehring's were held in place to the north by artillery. At this point neither side had the advantage, though the DAK's serviceable tanks numbers were now reduced to twenty-six.

By 3 July the Germans were now starting to feel the effects of the battle; exhaustion and dwindling supplies, as well as the effects of well-coordinated Allied artillery and air support,

were taking their toll. The prize of the Suez Canal was slipping further from Rommel's grasp and he was faced with some hard choices. To buy valuable time he replaced exhausted DAK troops with fresh Italian infantry and established new defensive positions protected by minefields.

Italian Semovente 75/18. These tanks, although bravely crewed, stood little chance against improved British anti-tank guns later in the El Alamein battles. (German Federal Archives)

Meanwhile Auchinleck, driven by political pressure from Churchill, planned to take the fight to Panzerarmee Afrika, but like the Germans, Allied troops were starting to feel fatigued and 4 July was a day of mixed results. A slightly reinforced XIII Corps advanced towards Panzerarmee Afrika from the south, but was met almost immediately by an effective anti-tank screen. To the south exhausted troops engaged with the enemy in a series of somewhat unenthusiastic attacks, which somehow managed to remove most of the enemy forces from the ridge.

A Valentine tank carrying Scottish infantry pushes on. (HMSO)

Auchinleck then shifted focus to the depression of Deir al Shein south-west of the Ruweisat Ridge. Over the next few days the results of the Deir al Shein venture were lacklustre, maybe as a result of Auchinleck's desire to strengthen the north. Rommel surmised something was going on and planned an attack southwards. Thankfully ULTRA intercepts warned Auchinleck of Rommel's intentions. XXX Corps' new commander Lieutenant General William Ramsden was ordered to prepare a strike northwards towards the Italian-held features of Tel el Eisa and Tel el Makh Khad.

On 9 July Rommel launched a technically perfect assault upon the now-abandoned positions at Bab el Qattara with 21st Panzer leading. He then ordered the 90th Light Division eastwards to find a weak spot in the Eighth Army's southern flank. As the 90th moved the terrific rumble of one of the largest artillery barrages ever to take place in the desert could be heard as the

A knocked-out Italian M13/40 tank being inspected by a passing soldier, 11 July 1942. (IWM)

Rommel in his personal SdKfz 250/3 command halftrack 'Greif'. (German Federal Archives)

Australian 9th and South African 1st Divisions struck out. The Italians were taken completely by surprise with the Sabratha and Trieste Divisions being virtually destroyed. The Australians stormed forwards and at Tel el Makh Khad they were rewarded with a valuable prize; Rommel's radio interception unit. Rommel changed his plans and sped northwards towards the Alamein Box, picking up battle groups formed from elements of 15th Panzer Division and freshly-arrived troops from the 164th Division at Tel el Eisa. For the next four days both sides tussled for the feature, with the South Africans relinquishing their gains at Tel el Makh Khad due to a misunderstanding of orders. However, the Australians had forced a salient into Rommel's lines and held fast despite repeated assaults.

Auchinleck was now in a position to renew his attempt to recapture the entire Ruweisat Ridge. On the night of 14 July and with illumination and ground attack provided by the WDAF, XXX and XIII Corps assaulted the ridge. The assault cut through the defences of the Italian Brescia and Pavia Divisions. Rommel's minefields and a counter-attack by 8th Panzer Regiment slowed the New Zealanders down, but by the afternoon of 15 July a secure foothold had been gained on the ridge by Auchinleck.

Rommel counter-attacked the New Zealanders, who were pushed off the western edge of the ridge and lost their entire HQ, including Brigadier James Burrows of 4th New Zealand Brigade, to the advancing Germans. Rommel's attack only halted when it reached the boundary of 1st Armoured Division. Even so, Auchinleck still held half of the ridge despite Rommel's best efforts. The following day the tit-for-tat attacks continued with neither side making much headway.

On 22 July Auchinleck, who had continued to harass the flanks of Panzerarmee Afrika, attacked the ridge with Indian 5th Brigade and the New Zealanders to secure Deir El Shein. This assault ended in failure, with the 5th and 8th Panzer Regiments evicting both Allied divisions before supporting armour could reach them. When the British armour finally arrived they fell victim to German superiority, losing over 130 tanks to the Germans' three.

On 26 July the Australian and South African infantry pushed southwards once more through the Axis lines toward the Miteirya Ridge. Without the necessary armoured support, which had been delayed in minefields laid by Panzerarmee Afrika, the assault, like the attack on Deir El Shein, came to nothing. Auchinleck had no choice but to go firm and take up

Air Vice Marshal Arthur Coningham and Squadron Leader C.R. 'Killer' Caldwell, Officer Commanding No. 112 Squadron RAF. Behind them stand 112 Squadron Kittyhawks with the famous 'shark mouth' painted onto the air intake. (IWM)

and reinforce defensive positions. He ordered commanders to begin the tasks of resting, training and re-organizing, and consoled himself that the Eighth Army now held the western side of the Ruweisat Ridge.

For its part the WDAF had gained a great deal of experience and Coningham's desire to retain full tactical control of his aircraft had proved to be vital. A First World War fighter ace, Coningham demanded excellence from his subordinates, and recognized the power he had at his disposal and how best to use it. He pushed the development of the fighter-bomber role, which would help turn the tide of the battle. Throughout the battle the air support available to Auchinleck had been second to none with huge numbers of sorties flown each day. Coningham later worked hard to establish a joint approach to the use of air power with Montgomery, developing the Forward Air Control (FAC) concept.

Rommel, however, was now low on armour and had almost exhausted his supplies. He was also getting his first taste of defeat, with Suez was now beyond his grasp and the planned invasion of Malta, Operation Herkules, cancelled. This would allow Malta to grow as a base for Allied maritime and air assets, which would increasingly disrupt Axis shipping and air transport in the Mediterranean theatre. All the while Allied reinforcements continued to arrive at Egypt's ports.

The First Battle of El Alamein was over, and whilst losses for the Eighth Army were high, they had learned one valuable lesson; Rommel and his Panzerarmee Afrika could be beaten.

New Zealand Division cavalrymen awaiting the order to move. By this stage all sides were feeling the stress of battle and fighting was slowly ebbing away into local engagements. (New Zealand Govt)

The graves of two German airmen decorated with the insignia from their destroyed Stuka. (IWM)

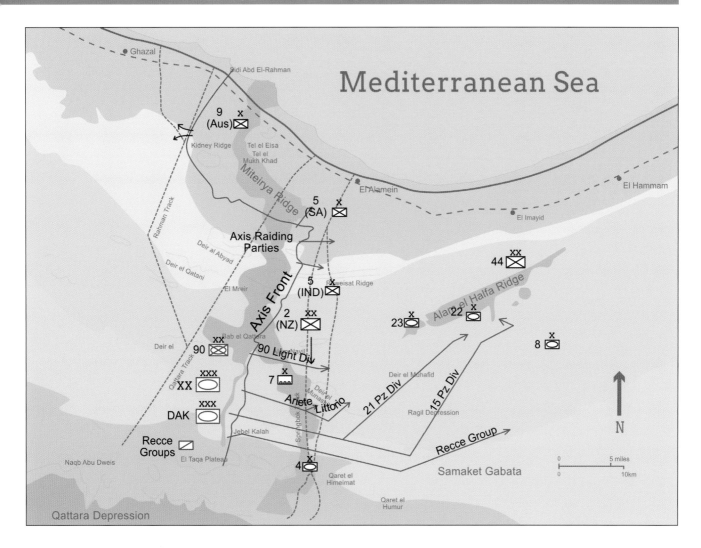

'Don't fight a battle if you don't gain anything by winning.'
Rommel

Rommel's supply situation remained perilous with the ports of Benghazi 1,300km (807 miles), Tobruk 640km (397 miles) and Tripoli an astonishing 1,900km (1,180 miles) to the west. Allied to this the WDAF had almost total mastery of the air and were ravaging his supply columns whilst the Maltese-based naval and air forces were taking a heavy toll of shipping. Rommel was still receiving troop reinforcements via the Crete air bridge, but it was ammunition and fuel he needed urgently as his armoured strength was slowly growing to some 200 German and 243 Italian tanks. For his part Kesselring could now call on 298 German and 460 Italian aircraft.

Major General Sir Eric Dorman-Smith, a master of intelligence interpretation, talking with the Chief of the Imperial General Staff, General Sir Alan Brooke, at El Alamein. (IWM)

A fairly new-looking Bf 109 receiving a touch of camouflage. These new arrivals would bolster Kesselring's Fliegerführer Afrika. (German Federal Archives)

On the other side of Rommel's defences the Allies had been busy. Churchill had grown impatient of Auchinleck's wishes to be given time to reorganize and retrain the Eighth Army before mounting an offensive in mid-September. After confiding with General Sir Alan Brooke, Churchill felt new faces and new ideas were needed. In early August Auchinleck was replaced by General Sir Harold Alexander as C-in-C Middle East with Lieutenant General Bernard Montgomery taking up the reigns of the Eighth Army after Gott was killed.

Train hard, fight easy. Crews climb aboard Sherman tanks of The Queen's Bays (2nd Dragoon Guards), of 1st Armoured Division. (IWM)

Montgomery soon became a popular figure with the troops, though he was considered arrogant and wasn't particularly well liked by many of his peers, traits which were tolerated given his success in the field. Like Auchinleck, Montgomery pointed out to Churchill that the Eighth Army simply wasn't ready to take the offensive. The reinforcements coming into theatre, especially those in the 'teeth arms', needed to be trained in the new way of fighting that Montgomery wanted. Nor did Montgomery wish to waste his precious armour, especially against the professional German and Italian gunners who were masters of the concealed anti-tank ambush. Ever the innovator, Montgomery also worked with the WDAF to strengthen the collaboration between air and ground forces. This new way of fighting was best summed up as 'Forwards as One', with no more splitting of divisions or effort. The Eighth Army was going to be better trained, better equipped and better led, attacking as an overwhelming force and only when Montgomery was ready.

Throughout July and August both sides paused to assess the situation and rebuild, ready to attack. Rommel knew time wasn't on his side, especially if he was to continue east. Meanwhile reconnaissance reports were unsettling; the Eighth Army was strengthening its defences from the coast to the Ruweisat Ridge. However, the area south of the Ruweisat Ridge seemed to be neglected, so here was where Rommel would strike, using the DAK as his spearhead. Its left flank would be protected by the Italian XX Corps' Ariete and Littorio armoured divisions, the right by German and Italian reconnaissance units. To mask his intent, there would be a series of smaller infantry raids to the north and troop movements would take place at night. Unternehmen Brandung (Operation Surf) would be Rommel's last large-scale offensive of the campaign.

Unbeknown to Rommel Montgomery had access to ULTRA intercepts, and knew that Rommel intended to take the Alam Halfa Ridge, south of Ruweisat Ridge. Montgomery immediately began to strengthen his forces around that area, drawing 131st and 133rd Brigades from the recently-arrived 44th (Infantry)

Division, as well as sending the divisional artillery to Alam Halfa. He then positioned 22nd Armoured Brigade at the western edge of the ridge with further defensive points west of Alam Nayil established by Freyberg's New Zealanders and 132nd Brigade. Finally, at the eastern end of Ruweisat Ridge, he positioned 23rd Armoured Brigade in reserve. To the south were 7th Armoured Division, 4th Light Armoured and 7th Motorized Brigades. These were to stop any enemy advance, but not allow themselves to be overwhelmed and had to be ready to attack the flanks of Rommel's forces. In the north XXX Corps and the Australian, South African and Indian divisions were held fast.

The one key obstacle facing Rommel were the vastly enlarged minefields which blocked his armour, and had to be cleared if the operation was to be a success. Rommel also had to address his supply situation by 26 August, the original D-Day of the attack, as he only had enough fuel for two days' action. Eventually Kesselring transferred 1,500 tons of fuel, which would give Rommel four days' worth of fighting stores.

On the night of 30/31 August Rommel's troops crossed their start lines, running straight into unmarked minefields whose depth almost brought the advance to halt. As engineers and infantry tackled some 150,000 mines an intense artillery barrage fell and WDAF bombers simultaneously harassed the pinned-down troops. The two brigades of 7th Armoured Division engaged the enemy before withdrawing as planned. By dawn the German timetable of advance was slowed by defenders more than ready for the anticipated attack.

Rommel's plan was faltering and two of his commanders were now out of action. Von Bismarck was dead and Nehring wounded, and at this point Rommel very nearly conceded defeat. However, news that a passage through the minefields had been found and the advance was continuing helped to change his mind. Given the delay, Rommel decided to push northwards before Alam Halfa, swinging past the edge of Ruweisat Ridge, before pausing to refuel and rearm.

A SdKfz 250 halts to allow officers observation to their flank. Note the Panzer III with its additional fuel canisters. (German Federal Archives)

Meanwhile Montgomery's defensive plan was working well, with the Italians and 90th Light Division bogged down. Even better Rommel's armour was advancing towards a cul-de-sac of steel with 22nd and 23rd Armoured Brigades and the New Zealanders waiting in hull-down positions and behind concealed anti-tank guns. The 15th and 21st Panzer Divisions were engaged by the defenders, who stood firm, inflicting a great deal of damage. By dusk the remaining elements of the 15th and 21st had withdrawn to resupply safely. Overhead the WDAF were dropping flares illuminating targets of opportunity for the following medium bombers and fighter-bombers. These attacks continued throughout the night.

The following day 15th Panzer tried to outflank the 22nd Armoured Brigade, but the 7th Armoured Division intercepted them and anti-tank fire stopped the movements of both sides. Meanwhile the Italian divisions were still trying to break through minefields but the defending New Zealanders were adding to their woes with accurate artillery fire. Rommel realized the attack was pointless and gave the order for troops to dig in and prepare for another night of air attacks.

Montgomery now focused on the area around Alam Halfa, determined to use it as a buffer stop. He brought 151st Brigade, which had been defending airfields to the rear, into the line as well as the South African 2nd and Indian 5th Brigades. Meanwhile the 7th Armoured were striking Rommel's eastern flanks and still the WDAF continued to harass the DAK, with support from USAAF B-25s, clocking up nearly 500 sorties on 1 September alone.

Rommel knew his offensive was spent and on 2 September ordered a withdrawal to the westward edge of the British

Defending the line. A South African sapper removing anti-personnel mines from their protective containers. (IWM)

Martin Baltimores of No. 232 Wing RAF flying to attack enemy positions. (IWM)

The new British 6pdr anti-tank gun would more than pay for itself in action. (IWM)

A final briefing? Rommel with Generalmajor Georg von Bismarck. (German Federal Archives).

minefields. This really was the last throw of the dice for Panzerarmee Afrika, and the dreams of capturing the Suez Canal went with it. As he withdrew, unaware of the ULTRA intercepts, Rommel felt air superiority had stopped his advance. To counter this he ensured his forces were dispersed whenever they travelled or laagered.

At 2300hrs on 3 September Montgomery committed the New Zealanders to battle in order to seal gaps left in the cleared minefields. The fighting was exceptionally brutal with the Italians and Germans counter-attacking the following midday. A second attack followed but was broken up by artillery and air support. Freyberg, keen to preserve the lives of his men, disengaged with Montgomery's permission, the gaps in the minefields still being open.

The Butcher's Bill was high; the Eighth Army lost 1,750 men, the Italians 1,051 and the Germans 1,839. Tank losses were also high with the Eighth Army losing sixty-seven, the Italians eleven and the Germans thirty-eight. The respective air forces had not escaped loss either with the WDAF losing sixty-eight aircraft, the Italians five and the Germans thirty-six.

Montgomery could now continue his work, building up to his mid-September offensive, taunting elements of Panzerarmee Afrika who watched bogus preparations for an assault from the south that would never come from the high ground at Himeimat.

A soldier stops to inspect the grave of a Panzer III crew, knocked out in the fighting. (IWM)

A SdKfz 10 mounted with a 20mm Flak 30 gun on the move. (German Federal Archives).

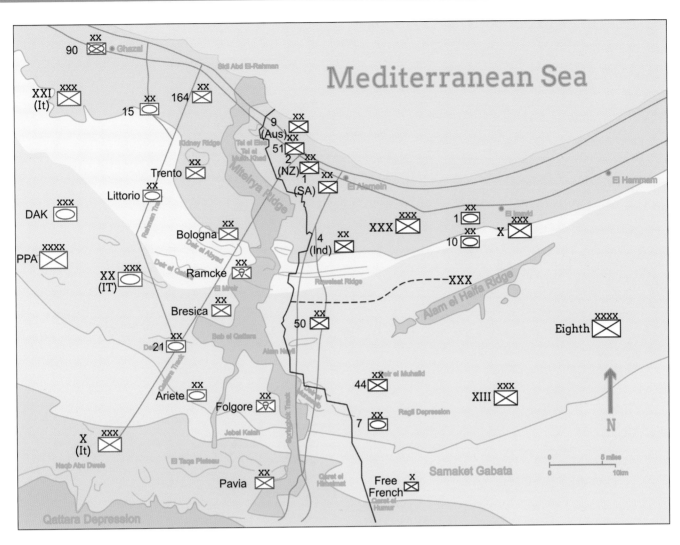

> Our mandate from the Prime Minister is to destroy the Axis forces in North Africa … It can be done, and it will be done!
>
> Montgomery

Montgomery felt that the Battle of Alam Halfa had vindicated his tactics and that the Eighth Army were ready to take the fight to Panzerarmee Afrika. Whilst defensive positions were repaired, training and rehearsals were the order of the day with every member of the Eighth Army perfecting their carefully-choreographed role in the ballet of battle to come. Now was also not the time to rob Peter to pay Paul and Montgomery ensured divisions would fight as such, with the full service support that would normally be afforded to them. Only the Free French and Greeks would be fighting at brigade level, and even then they would, like the divisions, be fully supported.

Montgomery had recently established a mobile corps of armour or *corps de chasse* to be an offensive weapon, designed to take advantage of breakthroughs in the front line. Once through these would run riot, harassing enemy forces and taking advantage of the ensuing chaos to establish footholds. For this task Montgomery used X Corps, and placed it under the command of First World War veteran Lieutenant General Herbert Lumsden.

Grant and Sherman tanks began to arrive from the US, taking their place alongside British ones in the armoured regiments from the beginning of September. Such was the volume of deliveries that by mid-October Montgomery had over 1,000 AFVs at his disposal compared to Rommel, who was able to field just over 500.

The Free French had fought well against Panzerarmee Afrika. Now they were ready to take that fight back to them. (US Government)

The gun park also grew, with over 500 2pdrs, and almost 850 6pdr guns which equipped all of the anti-tank regiments. There were also over 800 25pdr guns along with 500 medium guns. When the offensive started these guns would fire the largest artillery barrage since the First World War. On top of these figures the Montgomery had 195,000 troops supported by a huge amount of stores that were easily delivered via short road and rail journeys.

Montgomery reviewed all the senior appointments within the Eighth Army, wanting only élan, innovation and drive; for

Shermans were integral to Montgomery's new corps de chasse *doctrine and they were worth their weight in gold. (IWM)*

those that displayed these characteristics came promotion. For those who were considered too old, tired or unproductive came the inevitable chop. Montgomery's approach was brutal, but he was fighting a new war which needed new ideas and new ways of seeing.

Coningham had been equally busy strengthening the WDAF. Now numbering 104 squadrons of RAF, Dominion and USAAF aircraft, it could face Axis airpower with considerable confidence. The WDAF would also take the fight to enemy ground forces, day and night, providing fighter cover as well as

ground attack and reconnaissance, all directed in partnership with ground forces. The Royal Navy would also play a key role in the coming battle, mimicking amphibious landings behind Rommel's lines. Montgomery had prepared a truly awe-inspiring battlespace.

All the while political pressure continued, urging the defeat of Panzerarmee Afrika sooner rather than later. Not only would this help hurry along the relief of Malta but also force Allied influence further west in Vichy territories. But Montgomery would not be rushed, and mid-October remained the time when operations were likely to start.

To the west Axis forces were suffering from low morale; constant harassment from the WDAF and Royal Navy interceptions that kept supplies low and, in the case of fuel, severely rationed. Manpower losses weren't being made up and

Gods of Thunder: A Priest 105mm self-propelled gun of the 1st Armoured Division preparing for action. (IWM)

To Bolster and Harangue. Churchill drives past the troops in a suitably martial Morris-Commercial 8cwt truck. (IWM)

Caretaker commander Georg Stumme in 1940. His period in command was eventful and poorly timed. (German Federal Archives)

Rommel had been sent on an enforced period of leave with General der Kavallerie Georg Stumme assuming command.

Before leaving, Rommel ensured that his forces were organized to meet the attack he knew would come, most likely in early October. He established a static line of defence capable of holding out against infantry attack until the arrival of supporting armour. The line was 7km (4.34 miles) deep in

South African engineers training with mine-detection equipment in preparation for the Second Battle of El Alamein. (IWM)

places and covered by minefields, anti-tank guns, artillery fire plans and armour. The defences were littered with company-sized outposts, behind which were minefields filled with almost 500,000 anti-personnel/anti-tank mines and obstacles. Then came the heavier anti-tank guns, with further minefields placed 2,000m (1.24 miles) to the rear. Along the edge of this were battalion-sized sectors with support weapons sited to deny freedom of movement to armoured incursions. Rommel's intent was to soak up the attack, with each band of defensive positions slowing progress.

What awaited the advancing Allied armour: the deadly 88mm in the anti-tank role. Note the amount of expended shell cases and the barrel in open-sights setting of this gun dug into a forward slope. (IWM)

In addition to his armour, Rommel could call upon some 100,000 troops supported by 350 anti-tank guns and almost 150 of the dual-purpose 88mm Flak guns. The line was held by mixed Italian and German units, where German experience would harden Italian fighting spirit. Behind the lines were 15th Panzer Division in the north and 21st Panzer Division in the south. In reserve were the 90th Light and the Italian Trieste Motorized Divisions.

Among the new appointments was General Lieutenant Wilhelm Ritter von Thoma, who would take command of the DAK from the wounded Nehring. His command would be short lived as he would be captured by Captain Grant Singer on 4 November. Sadly Singer would be killed the following day, prompting Von Thoma to write to his widow.

Montgomery's plan was broken into three distinct elements. Operation Bertram was a deception operation to the north carried out by Commonwealth forces. Here waste packaging and materials were camouflaged and made to appear like stores. A dummy fuel pipeline was also constructed along with visually modified soft-skinned vehicles masquerading as armour. In a counter-feint, armour was disguised as trucks and transported to their start lines without drawing too much attention from Axis observers.

Operation Braganza was a preliminary feint assault by 131st Infantry Brigade against the Italian 185ª Divisione Paracadutisti Folgore. The attack took place on 29/30 September with the intent of capturing the Deir el Munassib. The Italians fought well and successfully repelled the attack.

19

General von Thoma surrenders to Montgomery at Eighth Army TAC HQ on 4 November 1942. His captor, Captain Grant Singer, would be killed the following day. (IWM)

A Morris truck masquerading as a Crusader Mk III. (IWM)

Operation Lightfoot was the main effort, calling for Lieutenant General Brian Horrocks' XIII Corps to attack southward, feigning as the main effort to keep enemy forces pinned down. Meanwhile the main attack would take place westwards on a 16km (10-mile) wide front, led by XXX Corps. Infantry would clear routes through enemy lines, pushing on to a point codenamed the Oxalic Line, and allowing armour to exploit the area behind the gaps.

The infantry would advance behind a creeping barrage, widening breaches as they progressed, continuing to use artillery at a local level to overwhelm the defenders. The intention was that Rommel would release his armour to stop the infantry, only for it to be met by the armour of Montgomery's *corps de chasse*. Meanwhile XIII Corps would attack positions around Deir al Munassib, pushing 7th Armoured Division westwards, but with a warning not to get bogged down. Its task was to keep the pressure on and ensure the German armour remained in the south.

Once these objectives had been met then both corps would begin to wear down the enemy through crumbling operations, drawing enemy armour out for engagement by the anti-tank guns and armoured divisions. If enemy armour wasn't forthcoming then 1st and 10th Armoured Divisions, known as Hammerforce, would seek them out and engage accordingly to prevent interference with the crumbling operations.

Montgomery split Lightfoot into three distinct phases, taking place over 12 days; the break-in, the dogfight and breaking the enemy. On the evening of 23 October XXX and XIII Corps

'Sunshield' split lorry camouflage cover on a Matilda tank in the workshops at Middle East Command Camouflage Development and Training Centre, Helwan, Egypt. (Crown Copyright)

Under new management. Captured Italian M13/40 (far left) and M11/39 (middle and right) tanks being used by the Australian 6th Division Cavalry Regiment. (Australian War Memorial)

Australian troops emerge from the smoke, practising a manoeuvre that was as dangerous to friendly forces as it was to the foe; advancing behind a creeping barrage. (IWM)

For Montgomery El Alamein was an opportunity to let the armour loose. A Grant tank moving up to the front, 29 October 1942. (IWM)

British infantry advances through the dust and smoke of the battle. (HMSO)

A destroyed German 20mm anti-aircraft gun with a relieved-looking crew. (Unknown)

assembled at their respective start lines on the edge of the Allied minefields. At 2140hrs the artillery started their barrages, first with counter-battery fire then concentrating on the forward positions. Over the next 12 days over a million artillery rounds would be fired, proving the Allies had comfortably won the logistics battle. Overhead the WDAF went to work bombing previously identified enemy positions and jamming communications, adding to the confusion.

In the north, pushing west over the Miteirya Ridge, XXX Corps' Dominion divisions advanced. The Australian 9th Division faced stiffening resistance though elements did reach the Oxalic Line. To their south 51st Highland Division used its brigades to leapfrog over one another toward the Oxalic Line. Whilst progress was initially good, mounting casualties and a larger

British infantry advances in open formation towards German positions after the night bombardment. (IWM)

A 50mm Pak being prepared by German defenders: note how well dug in the position is. Axis anti-tank gunnery was highly effective throughout the campaign. (Narodowe Archiwum Cyfrowe Poland)

area of defensive outposts to engage slowed the 51st's advance. In turn this delayed the mine-clearing operations on the main defensive line. Without access to safe corridors through the mines 1st Armoured Division remained observers. South of the 51st, Freyberg's New Zealanders were led by two infantry brigades before his armoured brigade enjoyed the freedom of movement to advance onto high ground. A sound plan that had achieved its objects by nightfall saw these gains disappear after effective enemy fire had pushed the armour back.

Major General Daniel Pienaar, a veteran of the East African and Palestinian campaigns of the First World War, followed Freyberg's lead. However, enemy resistance stopped any advance by armour and forced the South Africans to dig in. To the south the Indian 4th Division was employed in making a series of distraction raids near to the Ruweisat Ridge. By noon on 24 October XXX Corps had breached most of the minefields and had a foothold on the Miteirya Ridge.

X Corps' armoured divisions, who had to clear their own paths through the minefields to engage the Panzers beyond, were not so lucky. Engineers worked hard trying to clear mines in hazardous conditions ready for the corps to advance at 0200hrs. To the north only one gap was cleared for 1st Armoured Division between the Australian and Highland divisions' boundary. To the south 10th Armoured Division could access a cleared lane within the New Zealand area of operations. Soon traffic built up, preventing armour getting to the front line. Those that made it were subjected to effective anti-tank fire and by dawn had withdrawn to hull-down positions or well beyond the range of the artillery.

To the south XIII Corps 7th Armoured and 44th Divisions had the same difficulties trying to pass through the minefields, with only one being breached. However, the attacks, along with those of Brigadier General Marie-Pierre Koenig's Free French, helped to confuse the Italian defenders.

Despite determined resistance, progress was made and Montgomery was able to keep applying the pressure on Panzerarmee Afrika, wearing away the infantry and drawing the armour out into open battle.

German panzergrenadiers waiting to move, supported by a Panzerbeobachtungswagen (artillery observation vehicle) II. (Krakow-Warsaw Press Publisher)

23

... on the 27th October, 1942 ... Lieutenant-Colonel Turner never ceased to go to each part of the front as it was threatened ... In one case, finding a solitary six-pounder gun in action (the others being casualties) and manned only by another officer and a Sergeant, he acted as loader and with these two destroyed 5 enemy tanks.
From the Victoria Cross Citation for Lieutenant Colonel Victor Buller Turner

By 24 October new issues were surfacing, the main being the flow of six divisions' worth of traffic west through the cleared bridgeheads. Montgomery was keen to keep going and 51st Highland Division pushed on to help clear passages for 1st Armoured Division. Meanwhile the New Zealanders pushed southwards from the Miteirya Ridge supported by 10th Armoured Division and artillery. Now the Australians and South Africans began their crumbling operations whilst 7th Armoured Division was still trying to pass through the second minefield. If they were unable to do so, a night attack by 44th Division was ordered to force a gap. Overhead Coningham's air support continued to harass the Axis lines, flying over 1,000 sorties. For the defenders on the ground the inferno continued. Montgomery's attack had achieved complete surprise.

Desperate to get an idea of the situation, Stumme drove to the front lines to make an assessment. Nearing the front he died of a heart attack as Australian artillery shelled his transport. Von Thoma now assumed command of Panzerarmee Afrika and began counter-attacking at a local level. The OKW were aghast and Rommel was called back from leave to take command of the rapidly deteriorating situation. He arrived later the following day.

Trying to stem the tide. Italian infantry are transported to strengthen the front. (Italian Govt)

As the day progressed movement was reduced, with defensive minefields preventing the armour from breaking out into the rear areas to create havoc. The 51st Division pushed on to forge a passage through for the 1st Armoured Division, but numbers breaking though were low and their objective, Kidney Ridge, remained out of reach. No matter how hard Montgomery pushed his commanders to breach the minefields, they made little effort to try to break out. This lack of urgency was infuriating the ever-belligerent Freyberg in particular as his infantry's successes were for naught unless bolstered by armour. The 10th Armoured Division failed to support Freyberg for fear of meeting dug-in anti-tank guns and armour.

25pdr guns of the 2/8th Field Regiment, Royal Australian Artillery at El Alamein. The weight of fire delivered by the Allied gunners was simply incomprehensible. (Unknown)

The 10th Armoured Division advanced that night, supported by the guns of their own artillery as well as those of the 51st and 2nd New Zealand Division. Panzerarmee Afrika responded with counter-battery fire and air support. The ensuing chaos left the advance disorganized, and by the time commanders had reorganized themselves their covering barrage had moved on too far to be effective and the advance halted. Freyberg was furious. He needed the armour to support his infantry's advance, but what armour remained was either stalled on the forward slopes of Miteirya Ridge or stuck in minefields.

When Montgomery was informed of the lack of progress by 10th Armoured he urged its commanders on the ground to advance or they would be removed. Sadly these threats had little impact, with Freyberg reporting he was unable to start crumbling operations due to the lack of armour support. Every inch the warrior, Freyberg requested artillery support to help his division advance 4km (2.5 miles) beyond the ridge. Wisely Montgomery refused, knowing casualties would have been intolerably high without armour.

For his part General von Thoma was perplexed at the lack of drive by the Allies as it allowed him to strengthen his defences ready for an infantry attack on the night of 24 October. When it came it was preceded by the now-familiar huge artillery barrage, followed by a weak-spirited armoured attack. Von Thoma felt the Miteirya Ridge was the main focus of any advance and dispatched armour to meet the advancing Allies.

Elsewhere XXX Corps was progressing well, despite the poor performance of their armour. However, infantry losses were high, with no reserves available for the South Africans or New Zealanders to draw from. The unwillingness of the

A mine explodes close to a convoy as it advances through enemy minefields and wire. The minefields would create havoc behind the lines as divisions of infantry and armour tried to squeeze themselves forwards. (HMSO)

armour to fully engage could result in stalemate or worse still give Axis armour the upper hand. Montgomery reviewed his plan and made changes. The 1st Armoured would now shield the Australians drive towards the coast. Upon successful completion of this task the axis of advance would move westwards once more, necessitating another move by Panzerarmee Afrika's armour. The 10th Armoured would be

Whilst obsolete against Allied tanks the Panzer II could still support and secure the rear of advancing infantry and armour. (Australian War Memorial)

A CMP Field Artillery Tractor of the 9th Australian Division pulls a 25pdr field gun near the Mediterranean coast. (IWM)

withdrawn, with elements reinforcing the 1st Armoured and the remainder of XXX Corps holding Miteirya Ridge.

The attack began on 25 October with the 1st Armoured advancing, but anti-tank defences initially held them at bay, though armour-on-armour engagements saw the 1st triumphant. To the south 50th Division failed to break through the defensive minefield, but 44th Division held the ground taken by 7th Armoured Brigade. For its part XIII Corps tied up 21st Panzer and the Italian Ariete Division in the south. The night of 25/26 October saw the 51st push towards the Oxalic Line and 9th Australian Division push on towards Point 29, a rise which allowed for excellent observation. Supported by the WDAF, the Australians achieved their objective and dug in with access to the coast road.

Rommel returned to a desperate situation. The capture of Point 29 did little to improve his day and he immediately ordered a counter-attack, although the lack of fuel was now hampering mobility. The Australian defence plans, combined with superb air support and blistering artillery fire, soon stopped the attacking force. Rommel was forced to bring forward his reserves and position 90th Light Division in front of Point 29. Rommel also started to cast his valuable armour into fighting off small gains, armour he could ill afford to spare: 15th Panzer Division was now reduced to a mere forty tanks. Montgomery must have been ecstatic; his plan to draw Axis armour out into

Italian gunnery was amongst the deadliest encountered by the Allies. Often well concealed and firing over open sights, the bravery of the Italian gunners cannot be understated. (Archivio Centrale Dello Stato)

Reinforcements. A British soldier with his rifle and kit, newly-arrived in Egypt, 19 August 1942. Men like him would help swing the battle in the Allies' favour. (IWM)

British tanks advance to engage German armour. (HMSO)

battle as well as crumble opposition was working. Rommel, on the other hand, was slowly losing control of the situation in the face of a larger force; the numbers game was paying dividends.

Now the 1st Armoured Division turned its attentions to Kidney Ridge, a feature to the west. The 51st, South African and New Zealand Divisions cleared any remaining pockets of resistance before advancing those units who had not yet reached the Oxalic Line. Montgomery then formed a new strike force by removing the New Zealanders and 9th Armoured Brigade and placing them into a reserve with 10th Armoured Division. The 7th Armoured Division received a warning order to prepare to move north to join the new reserve, and 1st Armoured Division advanced northwards to draw out and contact any remaining enemy armour, thus relieving pressure on the Australians.

October 26th/27th saw determined fighting around Kidney Ridge centred on two key points of resistance, 'Woodstock' and 'Snipe'. These night attacks were intended to drive out enemy forces so armour could advance past both features safely. Supported by the artillery of X and XXX Corps, 7th Motorized Brigade advanced to contact in the north towards 'Woodcock' while 2nd Rifle Brigade moved south towards 'Snipe'. The 7th found their objective quickly, whilst the 2nd encountered stiff resistance from both the German and Italian divisions. The ensuing fighting was vicious, with both sides keen to take control of these two key points. By the afternoon of 27 October 1st Armoured Division were facing a determined armoured counter-attack with 'Snipe' bearing the brunt. However, the 2nd Rifle Brigade held out, defeating the counter-attack with valour and élan. By the evening both 'Woodstock' and 'Snipe' were reinforced by the arrival of the 133rd Lorried Infantry Brigade.

On the night of 28 October the Australians pushed northwards once more towards the coast road. While stiff opposition had stopped the Australian advance, it had weakened the German 164th and 90th Divisions charged with the defence of the area. By 29 October parts of 21st Panzer Division entered the fray from the south, and at this point Montgomery released Freyberg's infantry from reserve to clear the way for an armoured breakout along the coast road.

On the night of 30 October the Australians crossed swords with the 90th Light Division in a fresh assault, which propelled them towards the coast along the coast road and railway line. The Australians then turned eastwards to capture a point called Thompson's Post. Whilst not wholly successful, the attack created a salient into Rommel's lines, which made withdrawal exceptionally difficult for the Axis

Panzerjäger I, an example of a German self-propelled 47mm anti-tank gun, moving forward. (German Federal Archives)

troops caught within it. Rommel also felt that the salient could be used by Montgomery to form the basis of a powerful breakout.

Keen to prevent the destruction of his forces, Rommel pulled 21st Panzer Division from the battle and placed them in mobile reserve at a point close to Tel el Aqqaqir. The logistics problems continued to play their part and Rommel also learned that much-needed fuel was unlikely to arrive. Meanwhile Montgomery had once again changed his mind as to where the breakout would take place. For Rommel, who was certain it would the northern salient, the surprise would be total.

Abandoned German SdKfz 223 Leichter Panzerspähwagen fitted with a folding frame antenna for use with a long-range wireless set. In the background are three German 50mm Pak 38 anti-tank guns. (Australian Armed Forces)

If the British armour owed any debt to the infantry of 8th Army, the debt was paid on 2 November by 9th Armoured Brigade in heroism and blood …

Montgomery

Operation Supercharge was to be the coup de grâce for Panzerarmee Afrika and XXX Corps was centre stage, making an night assault with infantry followed by armour, whilst to the south Horrocks' XIII Corps would provide a feint attack. The main effort of Supercharge would take place 4km (2.5 miles) south of Point 29 supported by artillery and the WDAF. Freyberg's New Zealanders, supplemented by elements from 50th and 51st Divisions, would lead the attack. This time the assault would not have to contend with deep minefields, and once the infantry had reached their objectives the armour would take over the battle. 1st Armoured Division would engage the Panzer divisions supported by their anti-tank guns, while other divisions would continue to crumble away Axis defences, either side of the main advance, continuously seeking gaps to exploit.

At 0105hrs on 2 November Operation Supercharge began, with artillery pounding positions that had been subjected to nearly seven hours of attacks by the WDAF. The Royal Navy supported by simulating landings, adding tracer fire and flares to the cacophony of battle. The ground assault pushed against a 4km (2.5-mile) wide front to reach their objectives. Almost

A 25pdr gun firing during the British night artillery barrage. Over the 12 days of the battle the field guns would fire on average 102 rounds a day. (IWM)

immediately the armour got to work, and two squadrons of 1st Royal Dragoons pushed past the advancing infantry, going on to have a fine time creating havoc behind enemy lines.

By daybreak 9th Armoured Brigade of 10th Armoured Division had split into three and led the advance towards the Rahman Track in a bid to crack the defensive positions there.

Fire for effect. The night barrages were as beautiful as they were deadly. (IWM)

Tanks of 8th Armoured Brigade waiting just behind the forward positions near El Alamein before being called to join the battle. (IWM)

A knocked-out Churchill Mk III among abandoned Italian M13/40 tanks at El Alamein, 2 November 1942. (IWM)

A 'Vampire' sign outside an Army Blood Transfusion Service advanced blood bank in the Western Desert. These allowed dressing stations and mobile operating theatres to draw blood as required. (IWM)

Montgomery left the commander of the 9th, Brigadier John Currie, in no doubt as to the importance of his task, saying he was prepared to take 100 percent losses in achieving this aim. Currie and ninety-four tanks advanced shortly before dawn.

Advancing from the east they were silhouetted by the rising sun, making ideal targets for the anti-tank screen that waited for them. This screen consisted of German 50mm Pak 38s and Italian 47mm guns, as well as the terrifying 88mm in the ground-defence role. The ensuing engagement became the stuff of legend in cavalry circles, with the 9th Armoured Brigade reduced to just twenty-four serviceable vehicles, but achieving their goal and breaking the line.

With the Rahman Track now secure the 1st Armoured Division returned to the fray, but its brigades encountered strong resistance, with the DAK showing their quality on more than one occasion. The advance was halted, but only after heavy losses on both sides. The continued Allied pressure was paying off and enemy strength was weakening by the minute. The Australians seized the opportunity and broke out of the Point 29 salient, pushing north and east.

On 3 November Rommel tried to withdraw the Italian XX and XXI Corps, but an edict from Hitler forbade any withdrawal

A Churchill crew check their bearings whilst one of them removes tangled signals wire. This was one of six Churchills used in El Alamein as part of Kingforce, commanded by Major Norris King MC. (IWM)

The prisoner cache kept growing as the battle entered its final phase. (IWM)

and Rommel was ordered to stand fast. So Panzerarmee Afrika continued to fight, holding the advancing Allies for a further two days. Montgomery knew his plan was having an effect, but had no idea how effective it was; Panzerarmee Afrika was close to collapse.

By 4 November the retreat had started with the 15th and 21st Panzer Divisions falling back to a defensive line at Fuka. By dawn their transport was in full flight and infantry units that were able to break contact joined in the retreat. At this point the retreating Germans put their own troops' safety ahead of that of their Italian allies, leaving many of them to be caught by the advancing Allies.

Montgomery now released the 1st Armoured Division to fulfil its mobile role and once it freed itself from the traffic jams on the Rahman Track on the night of 4/5 November it set off in pursuit of the fleeing Axis forces. It was followed by 7th Armoured Division with the New Zealand 2nd Division who set off at dawn, and 10th Armoured Division also joined the chase. To the south XIII Corps advanced against fading resistance.

To the victor the spoils. Montgomery standing in front of his personal tank, 5 November 1942. (IWM)

Now this is not the end, it is not even the beginning of the end. But it is, perhaps, the end of the beginning.

Winston Churchill on the victory at El Alamein

Even now Montgomery's reticence in delivering the death blow to the fleeing Panzerarmee Afrika is subject to much deliberation; an act of carelessness or of honour and decency? Either way, by the end of November Tobruk and Benghazi would be back in Allied hands and an Anglo-American amphibious invasion, Operation Torch, took place in Algeria and Morocco just three days later, on 8 November. Rommel was now stuck fast and within six months the war in desert would be over.

Lance Corporal Charles Jeffrey, Private George McCulloch and Sergeant John Spowart of the Camerons, who all won medals for bravery at El Alamein, photographed on 26 December 1942. (IWM)

Eighth Army re-enters Mersa Matruh, November 1942. (IWM)

QUARTERMASTER'S SECTION

The success of every battle depends on a multitude of factors, of which command and control, logistics and training are prime examples. There is also the question of equipment and its effectiveness in helping the commander on the ground get the job done.

The Battles of El Alamein marked a crossroads moment for the Eighth Army, with domestic armour being replaced by reliable US imports. However, the Crusader was still fighting on and the workhorse of the DAK, the Panzer III, had been steadily improved with the addition of appliqué armour and an improved 50mm Kampfwagenkanone (KwK) 39 L/60 main gun.

In the air the Luftwaffe and the Regia Aeronautica Italiana were pushed hard, often operating at the edge of endurance from airstrips that were little more than scratches in the desert floor with poor logistical support. The WDAF was well equipped and supported with the latest aircraft, including the P-40D Kittyhawk, slugging it out against the superior Bf 109 in the azure skies over Egypt and Libya.

As modelling subjects, the Crusader, Panzer III, Bf 109 and P-40 are all well served by manufacturers, available in a range of scales and media. In the 'Quartermasters Stores' you'll find a selection of model kits and accessories in key scales. All have their merits with great potential for conversions as well as superb detailing. As new models are always being produced this list is purely contemporaneous and features kits that are available at the time of writing.

INTRODUCTION

A soldier refuelling a Crusader tank from a 4-gallon tin or 'flimsy'. These fragile containers would eventually be replaced by the more sturdy Jerry Can. (IWM)

The A15 Crusader belonged to one of three classes of British armoured fighting vehicles (AFVs) that existed at the beginning at the Second World War called 'cruiser' tanks. The Crusader was intended to work alongside 'light' reconnaissance tanks and 'infantry' tanks which were equipped with the armour and firepower to punch through well-defended key points. The cruiser tanks sat between the other two, filling the role of mechanized cavalry; armour protection forsaken for speed and firepower.

The Crusader filled a gap at the time of its introduction in 1941, replacing its developmental sibling the A13 Covenanter as well as the A9 and A10s in North Africa. Initially the Crusader was a shock to Panzerarmee Afrika, but this was short lived and by the end of the second Battle of El Alamein the Crusader was gradually being replaced by superior American imports, though some Mk IIIs battled on into Tunisia.

A pair of Crusader Mk Is in conference. Note the front MG turret and large single light on the glacis plate. (IWM)

DEVELOPMENT AND DETAIL

The Crusader was a development of the A13 Covenanter, designed and built by London, Midland and Scotland Railway (LMS) and Nuffields, to meet General Staff Specification A13. These new tanks featured the futuristic-looking Christie suspension which had impressed a fact-finding mission sent to Russia led by General Archibald Wavell. Nuffield Mechanizations and Aero were approached by the General Staff to develop a heavier cruiser tank to specification A15 weighting in at 20 tons versus the A13's 14 tons. To help spread the weight the Crusader was given an additional road wheel either side, and fitted with a modified 27-litre V12 Nuffield petrol engine generating 3,400hp at 1,500rpm.

The Mk III with its 6pdr gun extended the life of the platform long enough to see the Axis defeated in Africa. The camouflage is black over sand. (IWM)

The crew were protected by 40mm armour to the front and 30mm elsewhere; this reduced the weight to 18 tons, meaning the Crusader was able to cross the standard army bridges of the time. The Crusader also shared as many components with the Covenanter as possible, which meant features like the on-demand steering system and the constant mesh gearbox were common to both.

Over its period of use the Crusader was produced in three distinct marks; the Mk I and II were fitted with the Ordnance Quick-Firing (QF) 2pdr gun (40mm) and Mk III fitted with the Ordnance QF 6pdr gun (57mm). The Mk I and II were crewed by either four or five men and three for the Mk III, these changes reflected the development of the Crusader. For

A Crusader Mk I passing a burning Panzer IV, 27 November 1941. (IWM)

Cleaning the barrel of a Crusader's 2pdr gun, North Africa, 6 February 1942. (IWM)

a dedicated commander's cupola, the turret featured a single-piece roof plate that could be swung to the rear and act as a sun cover. The Mk III featured a split-opening hatch to replace the single-piece hatch.

The turret was a cramped affair with the Mk I and II having to squeeze in the gunner, loader and commander as well as a No. 19 wireless set. With the advent of the larger 6pdr main gun and the disappearance of the hull turret, the Crusader lost the loader and machine gunner. Now the commander was responsible for loading, commanding and operating the radio. The Mk I and II carried 110 rounds of 2pdr ammunition and the Mk III 65 rounds for its 6pdr, while 4,950 rounds were also carried for the BESAs, though crews were often able to squeeze in a few more cases of ammunition.

all marks the driver sat on the right protected by an armoured box, the front mounting a glass viewing block with armoured cover, to the right of which was a pistol port. In early models a simple machine-gun turret was placed on the left. Manned by a dedicated gunner, this turret was fitted with a telescopically-sighted 7.92mm BESA machine gun. It was capable of swinging through 150°, but crews often dispensed with the turret, which also removed the gunner, allowing extra ammunition to be carried. A BESA was also fitted in the turret coaxially with the main gun.

The remainder of the crew were the gunner, loader and commander, all shielded by the uniquely shaped turret, so designed to give extra elbow-room for those inside. Lacking

The Crusader was not particularly renowned for crew comfort due to its size and design deficiencies, meaning that the commander's views when battened down were little short of appalling. The original 2pdr gun was soon obsolete and its solid shot armour-piercing rounds would often shatter on impact against Panzer IIIs and IVs, much to their crews' dismay. Another more serious issue was ammunition aboard igniting when the Crusader was hit from the side. Investigations found that the issue lay in poorly-protected storage lockers, whose sliding doors were often jammed by the ingress of sand and dust. Subsequent retrofitting of armour alleviated the issue with little loss to the amount of ammunition carried.

Sadly the one round not carried, and often needed, especially when dealing with anti-tank screens, was high explosive. However, crews were inventive in their approaches and used the Crusader's speed and ability to fire on the move to their advantage, outflanking Axis armour. Enemy commanders soon adapted and often feigned a tactical withdrawal to draw the Crusader into the range of the vicious Pak 38s and 88mm guns in an anti-tank role.

A Crusader tank of 4th Light Armoured Brigade in the Western Desert, 20 September 1942. (IWM)

The crew eating breakfast beside their vehicle, North Africa, March 1942. (IWM)

The crew washing by the side of their vehicle, March 1942. Note the rough finish to the paint on the trackguards. (IWM)

Preparing a meal in the Western Desert, 20 September 1942. (IWM)

Nuffield Liberty L12 engine: note the individual cylinders, a design feature that would be a perpetual Achilles heel for the Crusader. (Stahlkocher)

Another major issue was the Nuffield Liberty engine, which was originally designed for aircraft. The Liberty was assembled not as a complete block but as individual cylinders. With extremes of heat, cross-country driving and battle stresses, individual cylinders would loosen, allowing the ingress of dirt and causing oil leaks. The desert environment also played havoc with the cooling systems which suffered from the ingress of sand which damaged water pump components and caused wear to the chain-driven fans.

By the time of its arrival, the 6pdr-equipped Mk III was nearing obsolescence as the 75mm-armed M3s and M4s began to enter service. Some Crusaders would stay behind after the surrender of Panzerarmee Afrika, bolstering the ranks of Free French forces. Later versions included an anti-aircraft platform, a gun tractor, which was capable of 50mph, and a recovery vehicle.

Crusader Mk I Specifications:
Type: Cruiser tank
Crew: 4
Weight: 18,812kg
Dimensions:
Length: 5.97m
Height: 2.24m
Width: 2.64m
Armament:
Main: 2pdr (40mm) Ordnance QF gun
Secondary: 1 x coaxial 7.92mm Besa MG, 1 x 7.92mm Besa MG in hull turret
Front hull armour thickness: 40mm
Engine: Nuffield Liberty Mark II V-12 petrol engine (4F+1R)
Performance:
Engine: 340bhp
Speed: 43kph
Maximum range: 322km

A Crusader tank being loaded on a transporter to be taken back to the forward area after undergoing repairs. (IWM)

1942; A Crusader tank with its 'sunshield' lorry camouflage erected, 26 October 1942. (IWM)

CAMOUFLAGE AND MARKINGS

Crusaders were fielded in an array of finishes with a base of sand or light stone. Occasionally camouflage would be applied over the top though later Mk IIIs in Tunisia were seen sporting various green finishes. Early marks featured the angular Caunter camouflage finish (1940–1), which was later simplified to a disruptive pattern of Dark Olive Green, Dark Slate, Very Dark Brown, 'Light Mud' or Black. Over time these finishes would be bleached by the sun and the abrasive action of airborne sand particles would fade their colours.

Late production Crusader Mk II, unknown unit, Gazala, May 1942. By the beginning of the Second Battle of El Alamein, most Mark I and IIs had been replaced by Mark IIIs, though some were held in reserve.

A Crusader Mk III, one of only 100 which fought in October 1942 during the Second Battle of El Alamein. These were mainly fielded in a supporting role whilst the 75mm-armed Shermans, Lees and Grants would engage the German Panzer IIIs and IVs.

QUARTERMASTER'S STORES

The Crusader is available in a range of scales. For the 1/35 modeller the Italeri kit, first released in 1976, remained the go-to model until quite recently, with moulds reboxed by Tamiya, Revell and Tomy. The kit has been adapted to provide the modeller with all three marks, as well as the anti-aircraft versions. The latest version (Nr. 6579), a Mk II, comes with an accompanying infantry assault team. Moulded in a variety of colours, dependent on manufacturer the kit also includes vinyl tracks and finally detailed parts, but the moulds are starting to show their age a little now. Decals are offered in a range of units, with the most common for El Alamein featured in the kits.

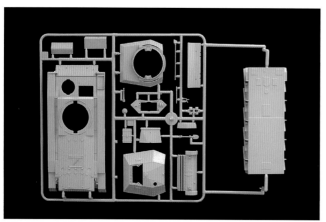

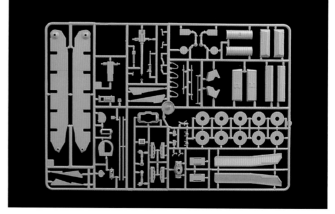

Italeri's stalwart 1/35 kit is still worthy of consideration.

To counter this stalwart Border Models have released a multimedia Mk III kit (BT-012) which is exquisitely detailed, featuring photo-etched details, a milled 6pdr gun, opening lockers and simulated weighted tracks. The mouldings are extremely sharp with well-observed details including casting numbers on road wheels, screw heads set at differing angles and finely defined bolt heads. Indeed such is the quality of the castings that photo-etch is used for those parts that would simply be too fragile if moulded in plastic.

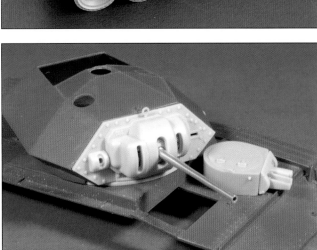

Border's new Crusader Mk III kit is awash with detail as well as photo-etched and metal parts what make for an extremely handsome model.

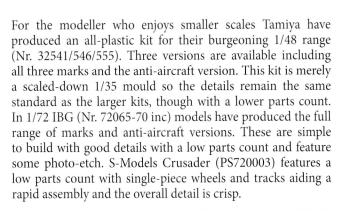

Panzer Art resin sets have set a high standard for resin detailing and these for the Crusader continue that tradition.

For the modeller who enjoys smaller scales Tamiya have produced an all-plastic kit for their burgeoning 1/48 range (Nr. 32541/546/555). Three versions are available including all three marks and the anti-aircraft version. This kit is merely a scaled-down 1/35 mould so the details remain the same standard as the larger kits, though with a lower parts count. In 1/72 IBG (Nr. 72065-70 inc) models have produced the full range of marks and anti-aircraft versions. These are simple to build with good details with a low parts count and feature some photo-etch. S-Models Crusader (PS720003) features a low parts count with single-piece wheels and tracks aiding a rapid assembly and the overall detail is crisp.

Panzer Art have treated the Crusader to a series of finely detailed resin kits including a stowage set (RE35-552), improved sandbag armour (RE35-625), and updated turret set complete with metal main gun barrel (RE35-178). Italian detailing concern Royal Model have produced a mixed-media set of detailing for the Mk I in 1/35 featuring a turned main gun barrel, resin hatches and photo-etched detailing (Nr. 384).

For super detailing there is a range of photo-etched and resin options available to the modeller to help bring their Crusader alive. Czech details producer Eduard produces photo-etched and turned gun barrels in 1/35 (Nr. 35279 and Nr. 34045), whilst Hauler (HLX48197) produces photo-etch for Tamiya's 1/48 range. 1/35 resin detailing can be found with Accurate Armour tracks (T46) for the Mk II as well as conversion kits for the gun tractor version with Black Dog supplying a set of resin accessories that can be utilized for all versions in 1/354 and 1/48 (T35090 and T48040).

For the 1/48 enthusiast MR Modellbau have produced two kits (MR-48043/44), one for the early Mk Is, which features the covered road wheels and hull turret, and a command version featuring a metal main-gun barrel. If you're after a simple modification then RB Model offer metal barrels for the 2pdr and 6pdr main guns in 1/48 (Nr. 48B22).

Hauler's photo-etched upgrades for Tamiya's 1/48 scale kits are as impressive as they are thorough.

The Tamiya 1/48 Crusader Mk II is every bit as detailed as the larger kits.

SHOWCASE BUILD

Italeri 1/35 Crusader Mk I (Nr. 6432), The First Battle of El Alamein, 4th County of London Yeomanry (4CLY), 22nd Armoured Brigade, 1st Armoured Division.

By the time of the First Battle of El Alamein the Crusader Mk I and IIs were 'yesterday's tanks', yet they soldiered on whilst replacement Mk IIIs and American armour arrived in theatre. This particular kit, whilst being over 40 years old, still holds its own. The detailing is still sharp and I opted to complete the kit straight from the box, finishing in pale stone to match 4CLY Crusaders that had survived the 'Gazala Gallop'.

In terms of build the kit is extremely straightforward, with some wonderful panel details; the turret weld lines in particular are well made. Interestingly the mantle shroud of the 2pdr isn't supplied which would mark this particular version out as an early Mk I. The gun has been converted to an early turned metal barrel from Aber.

The build is straightforward enough with no fit issues, which given the kit's age really surprised me. The only issue I had

was getting the tracks to sag; no amount of heating with a hair dryer would loosen the vinyl, so in the end I used a strong superglue to hold them in place. The antennas came from a dustpan brush and a short length of florist wire.

For finish I used Tamiya XF60 Dark Yellow, which was then oversprayed with a thin coat of XF57 Buff to simulate dust. Wear was kept to a minimum with areas dry-brushed and chipping shown with XF27 Black Green. The whole model was then sprayed with Vallejo matt varnish before a few details were picked out where the dusting spray had been a little too vigorously applied. The decals are those from the kit and well designed, with the colour balance spot on. Overall a great kit and one that really has stood the test of time.

INTRODUCTION

The Panzer III was the primary German medium tank at the beginning of the war, remaining in production as a gun platform until the end of hostilities. Although not produced in great numbers, it served a useful role within the German armoured columns in the early stages of the war, fulfilling its role as a medium tank well. It also proved to be easily adaptable with its main gun increasing in calibre from the 37mm KwK 36 to the 75mm KwK 37 as the war progressed. The Panzer III also saw its armour continuously improved throughout the war starting with a mere 15mm on early models and finishing with 50mm.

A fine study of a Panzer III ausf J at the Kubinka Tank Museum, Kubinka, Moscow. (Alan Wilson)

Early in the desert war the Panzer III was able to take the fight to the likes of the Crusader with relative ease with its short-barrelled 50mm KwK 38 L/42 gun. This was soon replaced by the longer 50mm KwK 39 L/60 gun which helped combat Allied armour. The powerfully-armed M4s and M3s then arrived whose 75mm gun could destroy a Panzer III beyond the range of its own gun. By the time of Panzerarmee Afrika's defeat the Panzer III had given a good account of itself, with the Sturmgeschütz assault gun variant proving to be an excellent anti-tank platform with its 75mm Pak 40 gun

A Panzer III advances past a burning truck. There's a wealth of in-the-field detail here for the modeller to soak up. (German Federal Archives).

DEVELOPMENT AND DETAIL

Designed and produced by Daimler-Benz, the Panzer III had its genesis in the massive rearmament programmes undertaken in mid-1930s Germany. These early AFVs were developed as part of a joint research project with the Soviets and the Swedes,

thinly disguised as agricultural vehicles, which would become the Panzer I and II light tanks. They were also used to train the new Panzer regiments in the tactics of Blitzkrieg, so that when suitable heavier tanks arrived crews would be well drilled.

The rare command version of the Panzer III, the Befehlspanzer III, seen with Rommel's personal transport 'Greif'. (German Federal Archives)

The new regiments would be formed of one heavy company (Panzer IVs) and three medium companies (Panzer IIIs). Initially the Army wanted to fit a 50mm gun to the Panzer III so that it could meet similarly-armed British and Soviet armour on equal terms. The procurement specialists at the Heereswaffenamt (Army Weapons Department) felt that this was unnecessary as the 37mm KwK 36 anti-tank gun was rolling off the production lines in ample numbers. This was the first gun to be fitted into the Panzer III, if only for the sake of standardisation of ammunition supplies. Whilst not an ideal situation, a comprise was reached and the turret ring was enlarged to cater for the fitting of a 50mm gun in future, which was installed in all versions produced from 1939.

Rolling on with Mersa Matruh burning on the horizon. (German Federal Archives)

The early Panzer IIIs, ausf A to D, were treated like prototypes, and powered by a Maybach 12-cylinder HL108 TR engine with an 246hp output. Subsequent versions were powered by the 12-cylinder HL 120 TRM with a 296hp output. Initially coupled to fairly light armour this gave the Panzer III an off-road speed of approximately 12mph, but a top speed of 40mph was achievable. A variety of road wheel and suspension setups were used in early models. It wasn't until the production of the ausf E that the standard setup of torsion bar suspension with six road wheels was established.

The Panzer III had a crew of five; commander, gunner and loader worked in the turret. The driver was seated in the hull on the left, with the radio operator/hull gunner on the right. Ammunition carried depended on the main gun fitted; early

Abandoned Panzer III ausf J at Sidi Regez, 1941. Note the turret bustle by the pup tent and the open hull side escape hatches. (South African War Museum)

37mm versions carried 120 rounds, with the short-barrelled 50mm carrying 99 rounds and long-barrelled 50mm carrying 78 rounds. By the time the 75mm gun was fielded the Panzer III carried a mere sixty-four rounds. Supplementing the main gun were the ubiquitous MG 34 7.92mm machine guns. Versions up to and including the ausf G carried two as coaxial guns alongside the 37mm main gun with the second gun deleted from later versions. A hull-mounted MG 34 was carried on all versions.

A knocked-out Ausf J decked with extra track draped over the turret to protect against air attack. (Australian Armed Forces)

As the war progressed it was clear the Panzer III could only be developed so far and the model was sidelined for the more flexible Panzer IV platform. By 1942 the Panzer III was operating as a close-support platform utilizing the 75mm KwK

An abandoned Panzer III ausf J on a trailer between Mersa Matruh and Sidi Barrani in Libya waiting for new owners. (Australian War Memorial)

37 L/24 gun. Various turret features such as the signal port were also eliminated and mid-production vehicles were given the same type of commander's cupola as used on the Panzer IV ausf E. Late production vehicles were fitted with wider 400mm tracks instead of standard 360mm tracks.

The Ausf Gs were the first to have the 'Rommelkiste' (Rommel box), a rear-mounted turret storage bin or Gepack Kasten. This was to become a standard feature on all subsequent Panzer IIIs. Panzer IIIs destined for use by Panzerarmee Afrika were given improved air filters and a different cooling fan reduction ratio. These were designated 'ausf * (Tp)', the Tp being short for Tropisch/Trop/Tropen (Tropical).

A series of contemporary studies of the up-armoured Ausf L Trop version. This particular tank was shipped to theatre aboard the SS Lerica arriving at Benghazi on 18 July 1942. Issued to 7 Kompanie 8th Panzer Regiment, 15th Panzer Division, it probably fought at Alam Halfa. After capture it was shipped to the School of Tank Technology at Chobham Lane, Chertsey, Surrey.

Of interest to the modeller was the arrival of the version termed the ausf L. This was an ausf J with additional armour applied to the front of the hull, surrounding the driver's vision port and hull machine gun. The gun also received extra armour with a wide plate covering the front of the mantle. Panzerarmee Afrika's Panzer IIIs were often festooned with additional lengths of track for armour, water bottles and jerry cans of fuel.

Panzer III ausf J–M Specifications:
Type: Medium tank
Crew: 5
Weight: 23,064kg

Dimensions:
Length: 6.28m
Height: 2.5m
Width: 2.95m
Armament:
Main: 50mm KwK 39 L/60
Secondary: 1 x coaxial 7.92mm MG 34, 1 x 7.92mm MG 34 in front hull
Front hull armour thickness: 50mm
Engine: Maybach HL 120 TRM (gasoline) (5F+1R)
Performance:
Engine: 300bhp
Speed: 40kph
Maximum Range: 165km

CAMOUFLAGE AND MARKINGS

Early DAK Panzer IIIs were often deployed from the docks still in their European-theatre Panzergrau finish. Vehicles would later be camouflaged by their crews using whatever paint was available. Once specialist paint became available the basic colour for DAK equipment was brown yellow (Gelbbraun, RAL 8000).

These two Panzer IIIJs were used by the 8th Panzer Regiment of 15th Panzer Division, which saw continuous action throughout the North African campaign. Vehicles were often unloaded and put straight into action, which was reflected in the finish of later Panzer IIIs which were seemingly delivered in Feldgrau and received a rushed sand overpaint before being deployed.

Panzer IIIA – Finished completely in Brown Yellow, this vehicle features a rather prominent red 15 Division Hex on the side of the turret. Note the DAK symbol on the upper hull side next to the driver's side viewing port. Also of interest is the lack of spaced armour for the immediate front of the upper hull, which identifies this vehicle as an early Ausf J which would have taken part in the pursuit of Allied forces during the 'Gazala Gallop'.

Panzer IIIB – Clearly rushed over from Europe to help bolster the DAK, this later ausf J features the spaced upper front armour to protect the driver and gunner/radio operator. The patchy finish is indicative of the rushed preparation for battle, with this vehicle being involved in the Second Battle of El Alamein and escaping to Libya.

QUARTERMASTER'S STORES

Second World War German armour is exceptionally well catered for by the manufacturers of kits, details and decals and the Panzer III is no exception. There are a range of kits that would appeal to the DAK modeller. Dragon have produced a

styrene and photo-etch version of the ausf J in the commander's version (Nr. 6544), As expected the kit is beautifully detailed with a detailed turret interior. Newcomer Rye Field Model (RFM) has produced a handsome ausf J version (RM5070)

The box art alone marks the new Rye Field Model ausf J out as being something rather special, whilst the interior detail is simply breath-taking.

featuring workable suspension and tracks. Like Dragon, RFM's kit features styrene and photo-etch which can model the up-armoured version with its spaced hull front and gun mantle armour. A full interior kit (RM5072) is also available, including a complete engine, turret and radio operator's section.

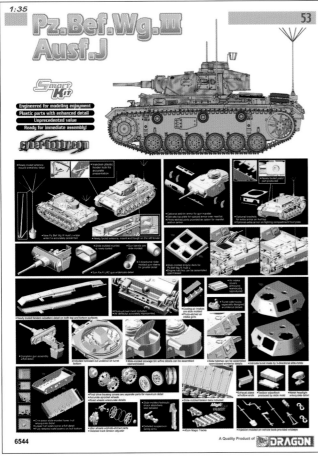

Dragon's ausf J features a huge amount of refinement, but the detail comes at a cost with the kit being intended for the experienced modeller.

Tamiya have produced a range of Panzer IIIs over the years; the first being their 1971 Ausf M/N (MM111) followed in 1997 by a new-tooled Ausf L (35215) version which still holds its own against more contemporary kits. Tamiya have scaled down the Ausf L to feature in their 1/48 range as kit 35524, which features a die-cast hull and plastic tracks, with very little detailing lost in the scaling-down process. Continuing the theme of kits for the smaller scale modeller, Italeri have produced a 1/56 Ausf

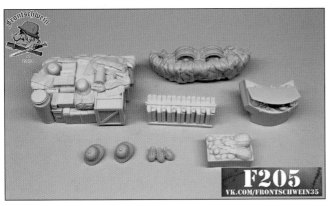

Frontschwein's resin set for the DAK Panzer III is beautifully sculpted and filled with details, including pith helmets. Not so sure about the pineapples though.

J as part of their Warlord series (15757). This features a good deal of moulded-on details, with road wheels moulded as part of the lower hull sides. With sympathetic finishing this will produce a fine model.

Another manufacturer in the popular 1/56 wargaming scale is Rubicon Models who produce an Ausf J/L version (280011). Whilst not as crisp as the Italeri kit, the Rubicon features a low parts count and clean structure that would suit a beginner or returning modeller. For 1/72 scale, Uni Models (Nr. 270) and S-Models (PS720016) offer kits with the Uni Models offering photo-etched detailing and both kits featuring plastic tracks. Both are great representations of the Panzer III.

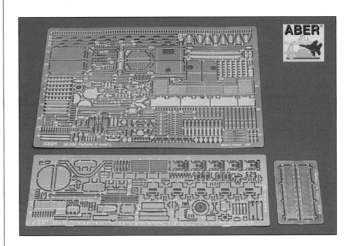

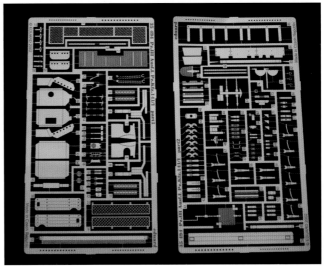

Aber and Eduard's photo-etch sets for the Tamiya kit are beautifully made, providing the modeller with more than enough metal to create a great model of the Panzer III.

There are a host of decals on offer, including Echelon Fine Details set AXT351025 for the 1/35 modeller, and Peddinghaus-Decals produce a sizable range of DAK decals for the modeller in all key scales including 1/35 (1083) and 1/48 (1084). They also produce resin details including a turret storage box (Nordwind 1/48 011).

For the detailing there are a range of options in metal and resin, including Aber's photo-etched detailing set Nr. 35038 which features a full suite of refinements including grills as well as turned metal barrels for the 50mm KwK 39 L60 (Nr. 35L65). Russian manufacturers Frontschwein have produced an interesting resin accessories pack for the DAK version which includes pith helmets, covered stores and a crate of food, complete with pineapples. For those wanting to update their

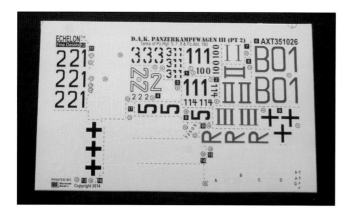

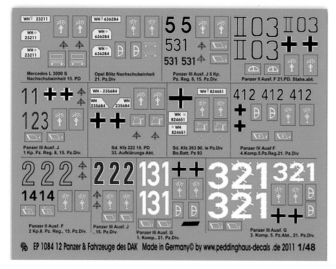

Master Club tracks are always worth considering, they're well made and held together with push-fit tapered pins.

tracks then the MasterClub Nr. MTL35009 tracks are worth a look. These white metal tracks with plastic pins are beautifully moulded and straightforward to assemble, adding an extra bit of authenticity to your build.

Echelon and Peddinghaus-Decals provide the modeller with a wonderful set of options for modelling the DAK Panzer III. Details are crisp and colours are in register with no discernible smear whatsoever.

SHOWCASE BUILD
Tamiya 1/35 Panzer III (Nr35215), Alam Halfa, 2nd Company, Panzer Regiment 8, 15th Panzer Division, Deutsches Afrika Korps

The ausf L version of the Panzer III started to appear in theatre from July 1942 onwards. Although it was quickly becoming obsolete, it could still hold its own against contemporary Allied armour. The arrival of the 75mm-gunned Grants, Lees and Shermans would soon shatter this dominance, however.

Whilst it is a little older than some of the others on the market it's still a great kit, easy to assemble and when complete delivers a brilliant representation of the Panzer III. I chose to use element from Eduard's photo-etch set (Nr. 35494) as some key details, such as grill covers, were missing.

Assembly is straightforward with some lovely details on the suspension particularly, I added power leads to the lights made from stripped sandwich-tie wraps and fine chains were added to a couple of handles on the rear recovery locking handles. Another detail was the antenna which was a length of shortened florist's wire. Due to supply issues I used the kit's vinyl tracks, which are more than sharp enough in detail, weathering them with pastel and pencil.

For finish I used Vallejo's German Camouflage Beige (70.821) sprayed over a black primer surface, with the larger areas receiving a little more paint. The model was then gloss varnished and the Echelon DAK Panzer III decals (AXT351026) were used. The whole model was given a wash of homemade grime before light wear and tear using Tamiya German Grey (XF63), and light streaking and dusting with a white/brown pastel mix.

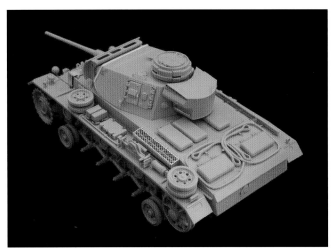

INTRODUCTION

The Messerschmitt Bf 109 pursuit fighter is without doubt an icon. The fact the Bf 109 would still be in action and production at the end of the war says a lot about its design, its popularity and its adaptability as a weapons platform. Some of the Luftwaffe's greatest aces flew the Bf 109 including Hans-Joachim Marseille, who achieved a staggering 151 of his 158 victories against the WDAF, including 18 in a single day.

A captured Messerschmitt Bf 109F in use with 4 Squadron, SAAF, given South African Air Force markings and serial 'KJ-?', at Martuba No. 4 Landing Ground in North Africa, January 1943. (San Diego Air & Space Museum)

A Bf 109E-4/Trop of JG 27 in flight, off the North African coast. (Unknown)

The Bf 109 was not without its foibles: the cockpit was cramped, it was renowned for its awkward ground handling as a result of its narrow track, and it was hampered by a limited range. The engine, although updated regularly, would find its plumbing easily damaged and low-level flight was considered unsafe. However, for some pilots to fly anything else was considered almost sacrilegious. Throughout the war the Bf 109 was developed and the design finessed to feature rounded wing tips, an extractable tail wheel, and an enlarged spinner.

A Bf 109F/4 Trop showing off its rounding wingtips as well as giving a good view of the cylindrical tropical filter. (Unknown)

DEVELOPMENT AND DETAIL

With nearly 31,000 units made, the Bf 109 was one of the most produced aircraft of the Second World War. Its origins lay in the pre-war rearmament programmes when the Luftwaffe sought to update their fighter force of He 51s and Ar 68s. Thankfully Willy Messerschmitt had been working on the Bf 108, a monoplane touring aircraft, which featured innovations such as mechanical leading-edge slats, and had a head start on his competitors Arado, Focke-Wulf and Heinkel.

After the trials, which took place in October 1935, the Heinkel He 112 and Messerschmitt Bf 109 were selected to progress, with ten prototypes of each being ordered. The Bf 109 was powered by a 695hp Rolls-Royce Kestrel V inline engine, with the remaining aircraft were powered by the 610hp Junkers Jumo 210A, the engine Messerschmitt had originally intended to use. The first three prototypes would also test various armament arrangements, becoming the Bf 109As. The remaining prototypes would be known as Bf 109Bs, with the B-1s powered by a 635hp Jumo 210D and the B-2s powered first by a 640hp Jumo 210E then a 670hp Jumo 210G. Deliveries to squadrons started in 1937, including the Legion Kondor in Spain.

Bf 109E fighters from JG 27 in flight. Note how effective the camouflage is. As the air war progressed the schemes took on a more universal grey look, with occasional embellishments. (USAF)

Five Bf 109s were also sent to an international flying meeting taking place in Zurich that summer. The aircraft performed flawlessly, winning the speed event as well as the climb and dive competition. These aircraft were fitted with developmental 950hp Daimler Benz engines. Aside from a forced landing which subsequently destroyed one aircraft, the trip went well; the pilot, Ernst Udet, was unhurt. However, glory was Messerschmitt's in November when the Bf 109 raised the landplane speed record to 610kph (379mph).

Production continued with the B-1s and B-2s superseded by the C-1 and the C-2, with their 700hp Jumo 210 Ga engines and

Brothers in arms. A Bf 109 E/4 Trop from JG 247 accompanies a Ju 87B from St/G 2. (German Federal Archives)

fuselage and wing-mounted 15mm MG 151s. By September 1938 600 Bf 109s had been built with Arado, Erla, Focke-Wulf and Fieseler producing units. The D series aircraft, which had waited for its dedicated Daimler-Benz DB600 engine, was short lived due to the engine's disappointing performance. One interesting feature of the D was the hollow propeller shaft and engine spur gear through which a 20mm MK 108 cannon could be fired. Testing revealed there were issues with vibration, which remained into the E series so as a result the cannon was rarely fitted.

The cockpit of a Bf 109 G-6/R3. Note the mount for the Motorkanone behind the joystick. (Smithsonian Institute)

The DB600 was replaced in 1939 by the more powerful fuel-injected 1,050hp DB601 engine which would power the Bf 109E or 'Emil'. The first variant of the E series, the E-1, featured two wing-mounted 20mm MG FF cannon and two fuselage-mounted 7.92mm MG 17s. By the beginning of the Second World War the Luftwaffe had more than 1,000 Bf 109s at their disposal with the E series being the only single-engined fighter used during the Battle of Britain. The E series was to develop into a range of production variants including the E-4

featuring an armoured headrest and strengthened canopy frame, and the E-6 reconnaissance aircraft. The E also received special factory modifications include the 'trop' variants featuring a special sand filter for desert operations, although it reduced performance by 5 percent.

Engine details of the Bf 109 F/4 Trop. Note how the large tropical filter housing fits away from the inspection panel. (Roland Turner)

The F series appeared from October 1940 and were distinguishable by their redesigned front and enlarged nose cone. These lost their wing-mounted guns and earlier vibration issues with the engine-mounted cannon had been solved so they now carried the 15mm or 20mm Motorkanone and were powered by a 1,175hp DB610N engine. A fuselage hardpoint was also provided which with a drop tank could give the F extra range or allow it to operate as a fighter-bomber (the F-2/B and F-4/B).

A damaged Bf 109F from III/JG 27 sits at Fuka, Egypt. (Australian War Memorial)

The G was the final version to see action in the Western Desert. With over 22,000 units produced, this was considered to be the summit of the Bf 109's design journey. Easily identifiable by the two large blisters in front of the cockpit to help accommodate the blocks of the two fuselage-mounted 13mm MG 131s, other

Wrecked Bf 109 fighters. the first fuselage wears the markings of III Gruppe (3rd Group) of a fighter wing, probably III/JG 27. An abandoned Messerschmitt Bf 110 also seems to be visible. (Library of Congress)

changes included strengthened wing structure and fuel tank armour. Powered by a 1,475hp DB605A engine the G was also available with a pressurised cockpit.

The ultimate expression of the Bf 109: A G-6 of JG 27 with two underwing pods carrying MG 151/20 cannon. (German Federal Archives).

In combat over the desert the Bf 109 had few equals, with the Spitfire not being available in numbers high enough to warrant concern, though pilots soon learned to respect the P-40's tight turn. By the end of the Second Battle of El Alamein and against a USAAC-strengthened WDAF, the Bf 109 ended the air war in the Western Desert a noble but defeated player.

Western Desert, Egypt, 14 August 1942: A captured Bf 109F ('yellow 5') of 6/JG 27 piloted by Lieutenant Gert Mix which made a forced landing behind Australian lines near El Alamein is prepared for examination by the RAF. Other German aircraft had tried to destroy this plane after landing in order to prevent expert examination. Hardly surprising given its excellent condition. (Australian Armed Forces)

Messerschmitt Bf 109E Specifications:
Type: Single-seat fighter-bomber
Weight:
Empty: 2,700kg
Max. take-off: 3,200kg
Dimensions:
Span: 9.92m
Length: 9.02m
Height: 2.59m
Wing area: 16.2m²
Armament:
2 x wing-mounted 20mm MG/FF/M cannon
2 x cowling-mounted 7.92mm MG17
1 x 250kg bomb
Engine: Daimler-Benz DB601 inverted V12 producing 1,050hp
Performance:
Max. speed: 620kph
Service ceiling: 11,000m
Range: 660km/1,325km with drop tank

CAMOUFLAGE AND MARKINGS

Throughout the North African campaign the Luftwaffe used a variety of paint schemes on their aircraft, often echoing the colour palette used by the Western Desert Air Force with use. Fighter wing Jagdgeschwader 27 (JG 27) 'Afrika' provide the fighter support for operations in North Africa from April 1941 to September 1942 and counted several aces in its ranks including Otto Schulz, Gerhard Homuth and Hans-Joachim Marseille. The Bf 109 was king of the skies over Africa, with the RAF unable to field Spitfires in enough numbers to take on this deadly fighter. Due to the loss of several key pilots morale in JG 27 sank and in September 1942 it was pulled out of theatre and replaced by JG 77.

Bf 109 F-4 Trop, II Gruppe, JG 27, Sanyet El Qotaifiya, Egypt, September 1942. This aircraft features a simple two-tone finish of Light Blue (RLM78) and Sand Yellow (RLM79a). The serial markings have been changes with the old serials painted over with a slightly lighter shade of sand. Note the Bear Rampant emblem of II Gruppe on the nose.

Bf 109 F-2 Trop, III Gruppe, JG 27, Haggag Qasaba, Egypt, August 1942. This III Gruppe F-2 features a random pattern spray of Olive-Green (RLM80) over its Sand Yellow base. The white fuselage band is wider than normal with the JG 27 emblem on the nose.

QUARTERMASTER'S STORES

The Bf 109 is an icon, and this is reflected in the thousands of kits, detailing sets and decals available today, leaving the modeller spoilt for choice. For the large scale modeller Trumpeter's 1/24 Bf 109E-4 Trop (02290) certainly meets the build bill. Featuring styrene and photo-etch as well as vinyl tyres, this kit is a great introduction to the marque and features a wonderfully crisp set of decals with two aircraft options. Czech HGW Models have invigorated Cyber Hobby/ Dragon's original 1/32 Bf 109E-4 to produce the E-7 Trop version (Nr. 103201). Featuring a mix of styrene, photo-etch and coloured placards this sharply-cast kit features a fully detailed engine as well as decals for five different versions of this famous fighter.

For those wanting a smaller-scale model, then Airfix's Bf 109E-4/N Trop in 1/48 (A05122A) is a great choice. Featuring fine details, the engine is moulded as part of the fuselage assembly, and the decals are sharp and allow for two versions to be modelled. Finally Tamiya's 1/72 Bf 109E-4/7 Trop (War Bird Nr. 55) is a wonderful little kit, made up of just fifty-five parts, featuring fine panel details and decals to complete three versions.

The modeller is spoiled for choice with a range of photo-etch, resin and decal upgrades in all scales. Eduard hit the ground running with their Bf 109E engine (Nr. 632137), designed to fit and replace the engine bay and engine of Eduard's own range of 1/32 Bf 109Es including the E-7 Trop (Nr. 3004). Other Eduard

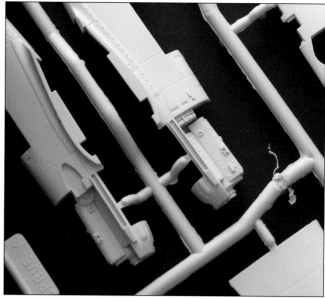

The Airfix Bf 109 E/4 kit is beautifully cast with crisp mouldings and wonderful details out of the box.

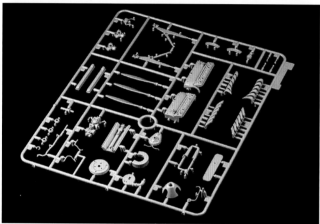

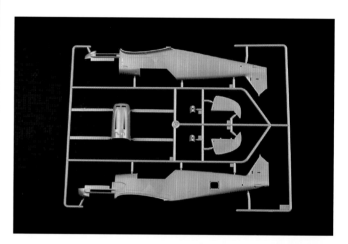

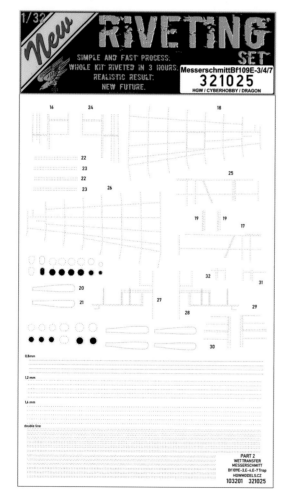

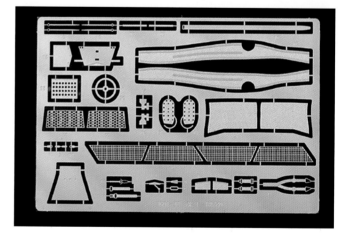

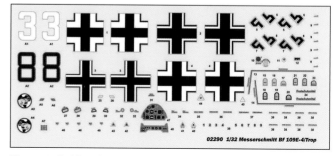

HGW Models' Bf 109 comes in a dramatically-finished box complete with a host of goodies to bring the kit alive including PE, canopy masks and positive rivets, which are added by the modeller to produce realistic rivet detail.

Trumpeter's 1/24 Bf 109 kit is awash with details, beautifully cut photo-etch and sharply executed decals.

items include printed cockpit placards and belts (Nr. 32777) for Trumpeter kits and a generic wheel set for the E series (Nr. 632004). An interesting innovation is the HGW Models' control surfaces fabric covering for F/G/K series aircraft (Nr. 321006). This set features a plastic frame around which a wet transfer is placed, replicating the real fabric appearance of all control surfaces.

For the 1/48 modeller Eduard have produced a replacement engine for the E series (Nr. 648474) as well as plentiful photo-etch sets, including Nr. 49525, suitable for the Airfix E-4. Quickboost by Aires have produced several resin update kits for the Bf 109 including an E series propeller, complete with pitch setting mount (QB48473) and early seat conversions (QB48525) for Zvezda's 1/48 Bf 109F-4 (Nr. 4806). This particular kit is highly recommended for the experienced modeller or one who wants a challenge. Hungarian multi-media firm SBS Model have produced a cockpit update for the Zvezda F-4, which features a wealth of finely sculpted detail and a single fret of photo-etch that will make the cockpit come alive.

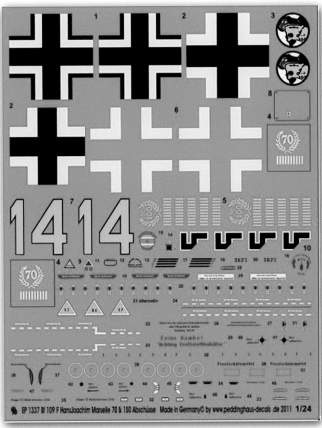

Peddinghaus-Decals are stunning, the yellows not too bright with all rendering perfectly sharp.

For decals Peddinghaus-Decals' 1/32 set for Hans-Joachim Marseille's F series (Nr. 1211) are captivating: the yellows are sharp, with no bleed on the Balkenkreuz whatsoever. For the 1/48 modeller, Kora models have produced two sets (NDT48021/22) of decals which cover the Bf 109 in the Western Desert, and provided decals and colour schemes for twelve different versions. Another interesting set for the modeller is made by LF Models, again in 1/48, and features captured Bf 109s in both original Luftwaffe and subsequent RAF or USAAC colours (C4827/28). This set is also provided for the 1/72-scale modeller in sets C7247/48 with the decals retaining their clarity.

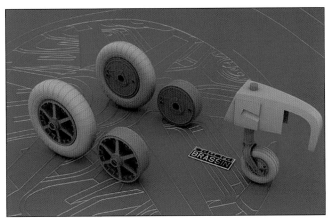

Eduard Brassin kits add an element of detail that is simply astounding.

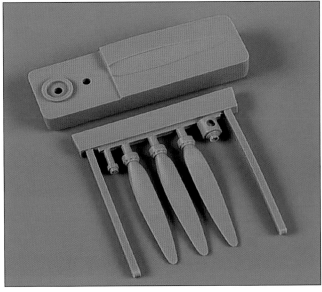

Quickboost by Aires' replacement E Series propeller set features its own setting tool.

SHOWCASE BUILD
Tamiya 1/48 Messerschmitt Bf 109 E-4/7 Trop, JG27, Libya, early 1942 – Andrew Newstead

The Tamiya kit is a very faithful model of the early war Bf 109 and allows you to make three different versions of the aircraft; two Western European aircraft and one Libyan example. I obviously chose to build the Libyan aircraft for this book.

Tamiya have a reputation for well-designed and engineered models and this is no exception. The kit's parts were excellently moulded and fitted together very well. One of the big surprises was how few parts there actually were in the kit but they were so well designed that a very detailed model can be produced from it. The only area that I decided to do any extra work on was in two parts of the cockpit, the instrument panel and seat belts. For these I used the Eduard etched metal set.

The model was finished more or less as it comes from the box. Tamiya provide markings and colour scheme for a much-photographed aircraft based in Libya from JG 27, known as 'Black 8'. The paint was done by airbrush, which particularly helped the mottled camouflage effect. After paint and the decals I used powdered chalk pastels to add weathering effects, especially exhaust staining and dirt kicked up by the undercarriage. A final touch was to use a fibre to make an aerial wire from the mast to the tail fin. An enjoyable build: even the extra detailing parts were fun to use and the painting was particularly satisfying.

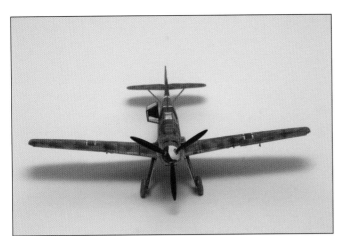

INTRODUCTION

The P-40 Warhawk was one of the most widely used aircraft in the WDAF with seventeen squadrons flying the type in various guises throughout the campaign. The P-40 excelled in the desert where it was able to utilize its low and medium level capabilities far more readily than it could in the European Theatre.

An immaculate 1942-built Kittyhawk at Temora, Australia, ready to take to the skies. (Chris Finney)

As Coningham's WDAF continued to develop the new doctrine of close air support the P-40 came into its own. In its role as a fighter-bomber it could carry a bombload of up to 726kg (1,600lbs) making the P-40 a formidable strike platform. Its rugged design, powerful punch and manoeuvrability, allied

It's more than fair to say the P-40 was a tough old bird. (IWM)

Pioneers all. Tuskegee Airmen in front of a squadron P-40. Location unknown. (USAF)

to its diving capabilities, gave it an unforeseen combat edge over contemporary Bf 109s which preferred to fight at higher altitudes. The P-40 was more forgiving to the novice pilot too, and as well as being well armed, later versions from the D onwards were fitted with armour around the engine and cockpit.

Although nearing obsolescence by mid-1943 the P-40 would continue to distinguish itself, especially in the hands of the famous 99th Pursuit Squadron, the first all African-American squadron, with Lieutenant Charles B. Hall making the first kill for the unit on 3 July 1943. The Tuskegee Airmen would continue to fly the P-40 into 1944, when it was supplanted by more modern types of fighter including the P-47 and P-51.

DEVELOPMENT AND DETAIL

Initially the P-40 was merely a radial-engine P-36 converted to an Allison liquid-cooled inline engine. At the time of its development the P-36 was the most advanced aircraft produced by Curtiss, who specialized in fighter/pursuit aircraft. It featured a series of refinements that helped it to stand out including being of all stressed-skin monoplane construction, as well as having fully retractable landing gear.

A study in design; UK military serial 'AK827' seen during maintenance at the Yanks Air Museum, Chino, California, showing off her cooling and filter housings as well as the fuselage hardpoint. (Alan Wilson)

The main driver behind the 1938 conversion was that it was felt that the inline engine was a superior power plant for a modern fighter. With plenty of examples to choose from, especially Schneider Trophy winners, it was felt that inline engines were the way ahead. But there were also downsides to fitting

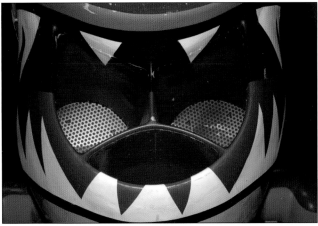

The shark mouth nose art so familiar to the P-40 and made famous by 112 Squadron RAF, shows the air filter covers and light wear around the cowling. (Roland Turner)

an inline engine, the liquid cooling system being vulnerable to battle damage, and they were heavier than radial engines. Curtiss developed the concept, and by using an existing and proven airframe was able to produce aircraft quickly, at a lower unit cost. The initial prototype, the XP-40, had its coolant radiator fitted beneath the aft fuselage. This was soon moved forward to its more familiar chin position so it could share the housing with the oil cooler.

In May 1939 the XP-40 was pitted against other prototypes as part of a pursuit aircraft competition carried out by the US Army Air Corps (USAAC). As a result the USAAC ordered 524 P-40s, the single largest aircraft order ever made at that time, and a year later deliveries were made to USAAC units. At the same time France ordered 140 P-40s, but these could not be delivered before France's surrender so were diverted to the RAF. There they became known as Tomahawks, where they established a role as low-level ground-attack aircraft.

Armourers demonstrate the load-carrying capacity of the P-40, by showing the size and weight of a 250lb GP bomb next to an aircraft already fitted with one under the fuselage. (IWM)

As experience was gained so the aircraft developed with the P-40C (Tomahawk IIBs) featuring self-sealing fuel tanks along with two wing-mounted 0.303s (7.7mm) being fitted, though these adjustments increased weight and affected the

Squadron Leader M.T. Judd, Officer Commanding 250 Squadron RAF, sitting in the cockpit of Curtiss Kittyhawk Mark I, AK919 'LD-B', at Landing Ground 91, Egypt. Note the red arrow unit marking over the exhaust stubs on the engine cowling. (IWM)

overall performance. In addition to these changes the aircraft were also upgraded with SCR-274N radio equipment and a 52-gallon (236-litre) drop tank capability which significantly boosted range.

As the need for more ground-support aircraft grew the P-40 was further developed and by mid-1942 the P-40E (Kittyhawk Mk I) was in available. Upgraded with a more powerful Allison V-1710-39 (1,150hp) engine, additional armour, and four wing-mounted 0.50-calibre (12.7mm) machine guns. The one area the P-40 continued to struggle with was its engine, which precluded it from operating as a fighter at altitude.

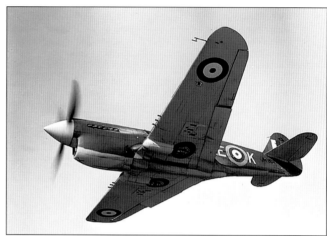

A wonderful shot of an early RAF P-40 in flight, showing off its wing form. (Canadian Armed Forces)

As a result of experimentation with the Rolls-Royce Merlin 28 the P-40 finally found the power it needed and Packard-built V-1650-1 Merlins generating 1,300hp were soon added to production aircraft, producing the Kittyhawk II. These aircraft were too late to support ground operations at El Alamein though some would later join the chase westwards and carry the fight into Southern Europe.

A P-40 from 112 Squadron RAF taxing across scrub. The purpose of the airman on the wing was to guide or inform the pilot of any obstacles, a danger when operating from rough strips in the desert. (IWM)

Even though it was underpowered for the first half of its career, Curtiss still struck gold with the P-40, with nearly 14,000 units being built between 1938 and 1944, with over 1,000 going to the RAF. Its tough construction and ease of maintenance gave it an enviable ability to operate from rough airstrips, with little support infrastructure.

Damaged P-40s under repair at a forward depot of the Advanced Salvage Unit. Note the hessian bungs placed into the exhaust stubs. (IWM)

Curtiss Kittyhawks of No. 239 Wing RAF fly into Marble Arch landing ground, past the Arco dei Fileni (Marble Arch) monument, erected on the Via Balbia coastal road in Libya to celebrate early Italian victories. (IWM)

Curtiss P40D Tomahawk Mk IA Specifications:
Type: Single-seat fighter-bomber
Weight:
Empty: 2,686kg
Max. take-off: 3,862kg
Dimensions:
Span: 11.37m
Length: 9.67m
Height: 3.25m
Wing area: 21.9m^2
Armament:
6 × 0.303in (7.7mm) or 0.50in (12.7mm) wing-mounted machine guns
500lbs (227kg) of stores on single fuselage hardpoint.
Engine: Allison V-1710-39 V-12 liquid-cooled piston producing 1,240bhp
Performance:
Max. speed: 538kph
Service ceiling: 8,900m
Range: 1,152km

CAMOUFLAGE AND MARKINGS

As with most of the aircraft used by the WDAF, the P-40 in RAF service as the Tomahawk or Kittyhawk was finished in a dark brown over sand finish for the upper surfaces and a light blue for the underside. As with most paints the finish came in a range of shades, which were bleached by the sun, faded by fine sand abrasion and worn by use.

250 Squadron operated both the Tomahawk and the Kittyhawk throughout the Battle of El Alamein, operating from Landing Ground 91 on the outskirts of West Alexandria. The Kittyhawk shown is in the colours of Squadron Leader M.T. Judd DFC, Officer Commanding 250 Squadron. Judd led his squadron on many ground-attack sorties targeting enemy airfields, supply dumps and motor transport, but they were also involved in air-to-air combat. On one occasion on 12 May 1942, intercepted enemy radio transmissions indicated that a large formation of Luftwaffe transport aircraft were heading for Libya from Crete. Judd took off at the head of his squadron and intercepted twelve Junkers Ju 52 transport aircraft 50 miles off the coast. He went on to shoot down two of them.

Flying Officer Neville Duke's Kittyhawk Mk 1, 112 Squadron RAF. 112 Squadron had been at the front of the air war in North Africa since 1940 where it had provided defence for Egypt. By the time of El Alamein it was operating its unique shark-mouthed Tomahawks and Kittyhawks in support of the Eighth Army. Neville Duke would survive the war with twenty-seven air victories as well as a DFC with two bars. After the war Duke would become a famed test pilot and would achieve the world air speed record in a Hawker Hunter (727.63mph [1,170kph]) in 1953.

QUARTERMASTER'S STORES

The P-40 was an immediate hit with modellers, its next-generation styling capturing the imaginations of numerous model manufacturers with wood and tissue kits from the likes of Joe Ott rolled out from 1940 onwards. This fascination with the P-40 has continued into the plastic age, with a range of kits being available to the modeller.

The Joe Ott P-40 kit was wooden and required the modeller to set to with a saw to cut the various parts out. A far cry from today's multimedia models.

The rare 1/24 version from Vintage Fighter Series is a nicely detailed multimedia styrene, photo-etch and vinyl kit. This is followed by a range of five 1/32 kits by Trumpeter which include photo-etch detailing and wonderfully crisp decals. Eduard released their own take on the P-40 using the well-received Hasegawa kit as a base, adding masks, resin, photo-etch and decals to further enhance the kit.

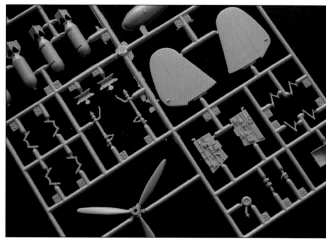

Italeri's kit features some fine details including separate cockpit wall detailing.

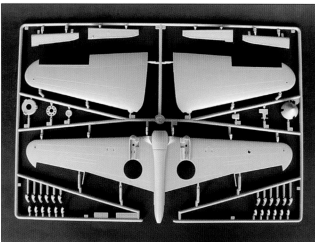

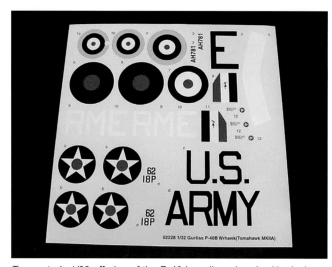

Trumpeter's 1/32 offering of the P-40 is well rendered, with nicely cut photo-etch and clear decals.

Several manufacturers have produced 1/48 scale kits including Academy, Airfix, Bronco, Hasegawa, Hobby Boss, Italeri and Revell. Two worthy of mention are the Bronco Curtis Tomahawk Mk IIB fighter (FB4007), a styrene and photo-etch kit. This features fine detailing along with decals to complete no fewer than five WDAF versions. The other is Italeri's P-40E (Nr. 2795) which features exquisitely fine panel lines and a beautifully-appointed cockpit.

The small-scale modeller has some great 1/72 kits to choose from, with Airfix producing a nicely detailed kit (A05130), though the high parts count is something to be aware of and this is the type of kit that will challenge the beginner. Other manufacturers include Academy, Hobby Boss and Hasegawa.

Hobby Boss's offering is worthy of note, being extremely straightforward to build featuring a mere thirty parts for construction and a straightforward but sharp decal sheet. Other manufacturers in the 1/72 range include Academy, Hasegawa, Special Hobby and Zvezda, with AFV Club and F-Toys offering 1/144 scale kits.

For detailing, the P-40 modeller will find the increasing popularity and sophistication of 3D printing providing a range of interesting updates including those from Model Monkey who produce a range of detailed gun sights (SKU24) and drop tanks (SKU48) in scales from 1/48 to 1/10. Another high profile manufacturer is Czech Master Kits (CMK) who produce resin conversion and detailing kits in scales 1/72 to 1/32. Their detailed 1/72 Allison V-1710-39 engine (129-7388) is worthy of being a kit in itself. Other kits including cockpit and landing undercarriage detailing, again all produced in resin.

CMK's 1/72 Allison engine is beautifully sculpted and would make a great addition for the modeller wanting to show a P-40 undergoing maintenance.

For photo-etch, Eduard, a name synonymous for metal detailing with modellers, have produced a vast range of sets in all the key scales. From accurately coloured cockpit placards, which include dials and straps (49786), to external detailing, Eduard spoil the modeller in super detailing parts (BIG33123). Other additions include white metal landing gear by Scale Aircraft Conversions (Nr. 48279) as well as finely detailed resin engines by Quickboost (QB48195) and the specific RAF pilot seat by Ultracast (Nr. 48257).

A great range of replacement decals are also available with Barracuda Studios producing a crisp set for the 1/32 modeller (BC32005), featuring the marking for three 112 Squadron P-40s. A similar set for five 112 Squadron aircraft has also been produced for 1/48 (BC48005) and 1/72 (BC72005). Czech decal masters DK Decals have produced a sheet for the 1/72 scale modeller, including a dedicated sheet for SAAF P-40s (72082).

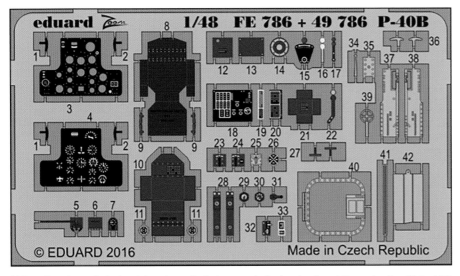

Eduard's coloured photo-etch sets really help a cockpit stand out and these for the Airfix 1/48 kit are no exception.

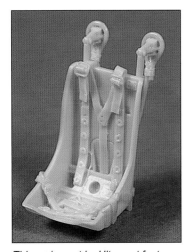

This resin seat by Ultracast features the correct period strapping for the P-40 in RAF service.

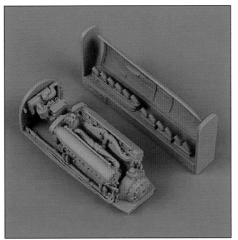

Quickboost by Aires offer this engine, which is designed to be used with the kit from Hasegawa.

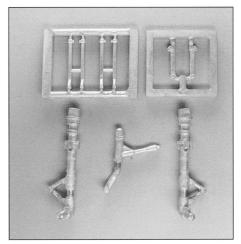

Scale Aircraft Conversions offer replacement white metal P-40 landing gear in 1/48 scale.

SHOWCASE BUILD
Italeri 1/48, P-40 Kittyhawk Mk III, No. 112 Squadron RAF, Nutella (Italy) 1944 – Geoff Coughlin

This Italeri kit, dating back to the mid-1990s, is a good base on which to build a decent model of the Kittyhawk Mk III. An added bonus is that the 2019 boxing that I've used here contains decals for a 112 Squadron aircraft with that characteristic shark mouth and its Dark Earth/Middle Stone and Azure Blue paint scheme – honestly, what's not to like!

The build is pretty uneventful and is well within just about any modeller's skill level. Detail is fine with recessed panel lines as well as options for stores: bombs and/or centreline fuel tank. I just used the centreline tank as I love the way the wings angle up and didn't want to spoil that by hanging two great bombs

beneath them. You'll need to find a seat harness or scratch-build one but apart from that there's enough detail for most of us.

Painting is very straightforward and I laid down the underside Azure Blue first and when dry, masked that out and sprayed the Dark Earth. I used thin strips of Tamiya tape to mark out the upper surface camouflage pattern before adding the Middle Stone. Galleria gloss varnish was applied in preparation for the decals then left to dry for a day, after which the decals and another gloss coat were added. Forty-eight hours later a flat varnish and a final weathering of oil wash and pastels were applied.

Flight Lieutenant A.R. Costello of Curtiss Kittyhawk Mark IA at Sidi Heneish, Egypt

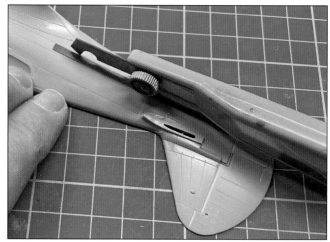

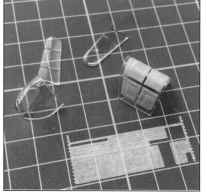

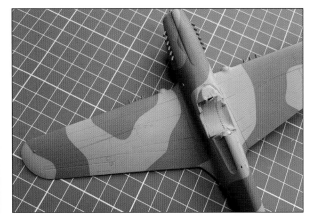

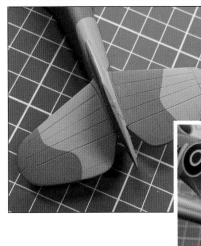

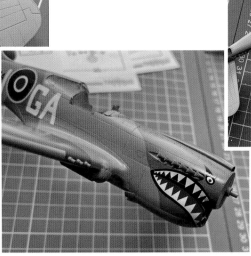

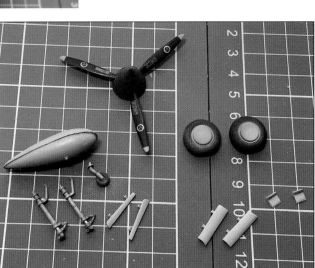

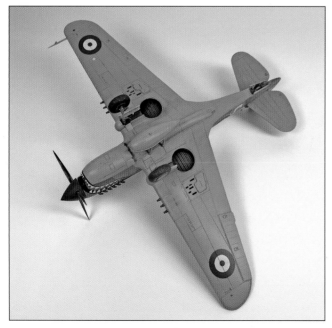
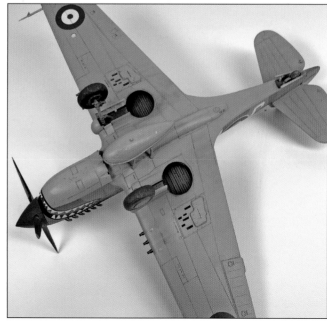